# ESCAPE INTO COTTAGECORE

**STERLING**
New York

An Imprint of Sterling Publishing Co., Inc.

STERLING and the distinctive Sterling logo are registered trademarks of Sterling Publishing Co., Inc.

© 2021 HarperCollinsPublishers Ltd

ISBN 978-1-4549-4443-0

Distributed in Canada by Sterling Publishing Co., Inc.
c/o Canadian Manda Group, 664 Annette Street Toronto, Ontario M6S 2C8, Canada

For information about custom editions, special sales, and premium and corporate purchases, please contact Sterling Special Sales at 800-805-5489 or specialsales@sterlingpublishing.com.

MIX
Paper from responsible sources
**FSC** www.fsc.org **FSC™ C007454**

Manufactured in Latvia

10 9 8 7 6 5 4 3 2 1

sterlingpublishing.com

Cover design by HART STUDIO

Cover images © Shutterstock.com

Contents, Author's own; Introduction, Author's own; p.10 (top) Rodolfo Marques on Unsplash; p.10 (middle) Sarah Le on Unsplash; p.10 (bottom) Alexandra Kikot on Unsplash; p.19 Tomas Hudolin/Alamy Stock Photo; p.22 Tetra Images, LLC/Alamy Stock Photo; p.26 (top) Calatorescu/Alamy Stock Photo; p.26 (middle) Eva-Katalin/Getty Images; p.26 (bottom) Carolyn V on Unsplash; p.30 Rafael Leao on Unsplash; p.33 Raychan on Unsplash; p.37 Author's own; p.39, 75, 105, 206, 212, 215 Hamza Khan/Alamy Stock Photo; p.41 Annie Spratt on Unsplash; p.45 (middle) Evgeni Evgeniev on Unsplash; p.45 (bottom) Gabriele Stravinskaite on Unsplash; p.49 Arthur Edelman on Unsplash; p.50 Leora Dowling on Unsplash; p.57, 60 (top) Author's own; p.60 (middle) Westend61/Getty Images; p.78 DEEPOL by Plainpicture; p.83 (top) Plainpicture/Juliette Chretien; p.83 (middle) Betsie Van der Meer/Getty Images; p.83 (bottom) Thomas Barwich/Getty Images; p.84 Markus Spiske on Unsplash; p.85 Plainpicture/Elektrons 08; p.86 Mikroman6/Getty Images; p.88 Plainpicture/Stephen Shepherd; p.106 Author's own; p.111 Plainpicture/Heidi Mayer; p.125 NightandDayImages/Getty Images; p.128 (middle) ClarkandCompany/Getty Images; p.133 Plainpicture/Caterina Rancho; p.135 DEEPOL by Plainpicture/Anna Kern; p.139, 146 (top) Author's Own; p.146 (middle) Plainpicture/Caitlin Strom; p.155 Annie Spratt on Unsplash; p.166 Sanuar Aktar on Unsplash; p.173 Annie Spratt on Unsplash; p.176 Tyler Nix on Unsplash; p.183 Christin Hume on Unsplash; p.187 DEEPOL by Plainpicture/Alberto Bogo; p.196 (top) Sophie McAulay/Alamy Stock Photo; p.196 (bottom) DEEPOL by Plainpicture/ Debby Lewis-Harrison; p.196 (middle) Plainpicture/Narratives/ Emma Lee; p.203 DEEPOL by Plainpicture/Emil Fagander.

pp. 14, 21, 29, 42, 45 (top), 60 (bottom), 64, 65, 67, 69, 73, 76, 81, 90, 93, 95, 101, 102, 108, 114, 115, 117 ,119, 128, 136, 143, 146 (bottom), 149, 153, 157, 161, 162, 165, 168, 178, 180, 189, 191, 193, 195, 204, 205,207, 208, 209, 210, 211, 213, 214, 216, 217, 218, 219 Shutterstock.com

# ESCAPE
# INTO
# COTTAGECORE

*Embrace cozy
countryside comfort
in your everyday*

RAMONA
JONES

STERLING
New York

# CONTENTS

# INTRODUCTION

# INTRODUCTION

I can thank my granddad for my love of nostalgia. Whenever my mum needed a break from the combined demands of childrearing and office life, she would drop my little sister and me off at Granddad's gate, and we would stay at his place for the weekend. Every creaking floorboard and dusty vintage book there was a comfort, and I knew we'd be in for a few days of magic and exploration. It wasn't uncommon for the other grandchildren to end up there too. Together, the six of us would rummage through the attic in search of antique treasure and my grandma's old vintage dresses, sneak off to neighboring orchards and pinch apples, round up the geese and collect their eggs for breakfast. And if it was raining, we would huddle around the range cooker and exchange anecdotes and tales.

School was difficult for me. I struggled with sensory and social issues and minimal support, and by the time I reached secondary school, my mental health was at a crisis point. All through this time, I knew I would be safe when I got to Granddad's house. I could play in the garden on my

own without judgement, or lose myself in a storybook while Granddad kept the fire stocked with logs. It was a haven from the rest of the world and the first place I felt truly able to be myself.

Granddad's place somehow managed to lag behind advances in technology. When mobile phones became the norm, they wouldn't work in his village. Broadband lines were installed for many of us, but not for him. My coziest memory is of staying in an old pine bed in "the Blue bedroom" as a teenager. I realized that due to the lack of signal, there was no possibility of returning my friends' text messages, and I settled instead on watching the raindrops as they made patterns on the window. The ambient buzz of the house, the warm flicker of light from the lamp on the nightstand and the occasional hoot of an owl took me away from my stress and lulled me into a gentle calm. Having no choice but to observe, I learned how restorative nature, solitude, and quiet could be.

Although my memories of being dropped off at Granddad's house are a few decades old now, they still bring me the same sense of enchantment. I've woven as many strands of them into my adult life as I possibly can: I still replenish lost energy with walks in nature, I search flea markets for dresses reminiscent of my grandma and I decorate my home with old books and antiques that bring me a gentle reminder to live slowly and intentionally. With these actions, I restore a sense of safety for myself that the world can otherwise deplete.

In today's fast-paced times, where productivity is valued over contentment, many of us are longing for old-fashioned comforts and a safe space to explore our identities. That's where Cottagecore comes in.

Cottagecore isn't about moving to a large estate in the country, nor is it a title that's earned from owning land. Cottagecore is an internet aesthetic, inspired by the nostalgia of rural life. It values traditions such as crafts, baking, preserving the natural world and caring for others. As Cottagecore was founded by the LGBQTIA+ community, it seeks to make a safe space where pastoral comforts can be enjoyed by all. Imagine a life where you avoid all of your stresses, relocate to a fairy-tale cabin in the woods, and write your own narrative among nature. That escapism is the essence of Cottagecore—taking comforting aspects of the past and tying them in with modern existence to create a sense of magic and escape.

Cottage life has had many different meanings throughout its history. The earliest cottages of medieval England were built on the grounds of manor houses as residences for workers, who would work full-time to comply with orders from the lord of the manor. These early cottages were simple dwellings, built from local materials and designed to meet only the most basic needs. There would have been a smallholding for the owner to raise animals or grow food and medicinal herbs, but there was no scope for the fanciful decorations and colorful cottage gardens that we know today. The goal of the cottage dweller at this point was survival, so there really weren't any frills attached to the lifestyle.

Life for the cottager had begun to look more promising by the sixteenth century, when Queen Elizabeth I set about improving the lives of the poor. Many comfortable timber-framed English cottages were built during her reign. It is these that come to mind when we think of idealized rural life—a modestly sized detached dwelling with exposed timber beams, tall chimney stacks extending from the hearth, charming timber-framed windows, a thatched roof and a garden full of trees, shrubs, and herbs. The sort of cottage we might think of as belonging in a fairy tale or bedtime story. This provided the origins for the romanticized view of cottage life.

By the eighteenth century, cottages were built to house miners and weavers, designs were sophisticated, but functionality was still a priority. Cottages were often built to a "two-up, two-down" plan, meaning there were two rooms upstairs and two rooms downstairs, and terraced building was common.

From the Victorian era, industrialization and mass production freed cottage owners from the need to be self-sufficient. Many people abandoned their rural lives to work in the city. For those who remained, gardens became increasingly ornamental, and interiors more fashionable. Throughout the era, cottage life came to be associated with flowers, abundance, and affluence.

The history of cottage life might have stopped there, but with the arrival of Cottagecore, we have been able to update things a bit. Cottage life is no longer reserved for those who own a cottage. Instead, it is becoming a lifestyle or a hobby that can be enjoyed in both the city and the country. We are free to enjoy walks among trees, baking at home or listening to folk music. Cottagecore is about appreciating simple pleasures that bring us safety and joy.

By combining past and present, we can replace problematic and binary values, while maintaining an appreciation for the beautiful— whether it's a love of vintage fabric, growing herbs on a windowsill or simply finding the time to read a book in an outdoor space. Thankfully,

we have also gained the ability to capture and share our love of the whimsical through photos and social media, which has inspired many to add a little Cottagecore to their own experience.

This book isn't about uprooting your life in the city and settling off-grid in the middle of nowhere; nor is it about an unattainable or prescriptive lifestyle. It's not even about living in a cottage. It's an exploration of the different aspects of Cottagecore, including relaxation, home decorating, style, gardening, food, travel, and community. It will help you notice seasonal change and rekindle your love of nature. You are free to experiment with as many or as few ideas as you wish. Just let them bring you a nostalgic sense of joy as you escape into the magic of Cottagecore.

# MINDFULNESS

# MINDFULNESS

Many of us dream of moving to the countryside and escaping the rat race of working life. We envision a slow lifestyle that's full of simple and rewarding tasks. Instead of our morning commute, we might stroll through a garden and collect eggs from a chicken coop. The day would be structured around walks in nature, and in the evening we might cozy up by the fireside. The aim being to escape stress and feel connected with nature and the present moment.

Cottagecore is about bringing a sense of peace and contentment into our everyday lives, wherever we find ourselves. Thankfully, there are plenty of ways we can connect with the present moment and feel more grounded.

Mindfulness is built upon teachings of the Eastern world and has roots in a number of religions. Many Western authorities in mindfulness learned from Buddhist teachers, and some therefore consider mindfulness to be a simplified representation of sati, the first step towards enlightenment in Buddhism. Sati has a broad meaning

within Buddhism. It has been translated to encompass a number of elements, generally summarized as concentrated attention. Although in the West we often practice mindfulness as a discipline in its own right, it is important to remember that its origins lie within religion.

Mindfulness can be practiced in a number of ways, from simple breathing exercises to guided forest bathing (the Japanese ritual of being calm and quiet among the trees, while breathing deeply—see p. 126). The overall goal is to bring your attention to the present moment without judgement, to let go of the past and stop worrying about the future. Mindfulness is a practice of observation and acceptance. There are so many benefits associated with it. Studies have shown that it has the ability to reduce symptoms of stress, depression and anxiety. Just a short session can have long-lasting, positive effects on the way we experience the world.

Because we approach mindfulness without judgement, we should try not to get too hung up on the end result. Instead, we should allow ourselves to experience the process without focusing too much on our skill level.

"Do not dwell in
the past, do not
dream of the future,
concentrate the
mind on the
present moment."

– Buddha –

# Breathing exercises

The most straightforward form of mindfulness requires nothing but your breath. Breathing exercises are useful tools for combatting stress and anxiety, and grounding yourself in the present moment. They provide a sense of connection between the mind and body that often gets lost in the chaos of modern life. Once you have tried these exercises a few times, you will always have them with you to use whenever you need a moment of calm and connection.

To ease yourself into breathing exercises, begin with a couple of minutes per day. You can increase this amount of time as you desire, and practice at multiple moments throughout the day, whenever you feel your body or mind needs it.

You can do these exercises either seated or lying down. If you are seated, place your feet flat on the floor and roughly hip distance apart. With your palms facing upwards, rest one hand on top of the other in your lap. Imagine there is a string pulling you up from the crown of your head; this will help you to settle into a comfortable posture—you want to lengthen the spine and relax the shoulders.

If you're lying down, move your arms slightly away from your body and face your palms up. You can either lie with your legs straight or bend your knees so that your feet are flat on the floor. Avoid wearing tight clothes that might interfere with deep breathing.

## Pursed lip breathing

This exercise enables you to easily take control of your breath. The deliberate control will allow you to slow your rate of breathing and feel more relaxed. It's a useful exercise for providing immediate relief when you are feeling stressed or overloaded.

1. Sit or lie down in a comfortable position (see p. 23). You may prefer to close your eyes.

2. Relax your head, neck, and shoulders. Close your mouth, and inhale through your nose for two counts.

3. Purse your lips as though you are about to whistle.

4. Exhale through your pursed lips for four counts.

5. Continue with this pattern for as long as you wish.

## Belly breathing

This exercise helps to restore a connection with your body. It can allow you to feel more grounded in yourself and in the present moment, and it may also help to reduce the amount of effort required of your body while it breathes. It's a useful tool for times when your thoughts are running wild and you need to collect yourself.

1. Sit or lie down in a comfortable position (see p. 23). You may prefer to close your eyes.

2. Rest your left hand on your belly and your right hand on your heart.

3. Find a gentle breathing rhythm through either your nose or mouth.

4. Pay attention to the rise and fall of your chest as you breathe. You may notice more movement in your ribcage and less in your belly. Encourage your breath movements to fill your belly by moving the area as you breathe.

5. If you notice yourself getting distracted, gently return your attention to the rise and fall of your belly.

6. Continue with this pattern for as long as you wish.

## Equal breathing

Equal breathing means inhaling and exhaling in equal measure, which helps you to relax and enhance your focus. Feel free to increase the breathing counts to achieve a deeper breath, provided your inhale is as long as your exhale.

1. Sit or lie down in a comfortable position (see p. 23). You may prefer to close your eyes.

2. Inhale slowly through your nose to the count of three.

3. When you are ready, exhale slowly through your nose to the count of three.

4. Continue with this pattern for as long as you wish.

# A mindfulness bath ritual

A long soak in a warm bath is a sure way to relieve stress and muscle tension and calm an overactive mind. There are a few little indulgences you can add to your bath to create a relaxing sensory haven.

Essential oils are a great-value way to personalise your bath ritual. These are highly concentrated, so you will need only a few drops and a small bottle will last for months. Each type of oil brings a different quality (see p. 28), so you can tailor your bath to your needs, whether you want to relax, invigorate yourself or simply enjoy a favorite scent.

Paying attention to the scent of your chosen essential oil is also a useful focal point for practicing mindfulness. All you need to do is guide your attention towards the scent. If you notice your thoughts drifting to other things, gently bring your focus back towards the scent again.

Before using an essential oil in the bath, be sure to dilute it with a carrier oil. This will ensure that it doesn't cause irritation. Vegetable-based oils are great for this; you might want to try almond, grapeseed or olive oil. Mix one tablespoon of carrier oil with five to fifteen drops of your chosen essential oil. You can either add this mix to the bath just as you are about to get in or try massaging the oil mix on to your skin beforehand.

# Essential oils for the bath

* **Lavender:** promotes relaxation and restfulness and is often used as a sleep aid. As such, it is a wonderful oil to use in an evening bath as you unwind and get ready for bed.

* **Lemon oil:** an invigorating scent that can be used to regain energy, boost mood, and reduce stress. Lemon oil is also used to reduce pain. There is plenty of value in this powerful essential oil.

* **Chamomile:** can be used for relieving anxiety and promoting restfulness, which makes it another relaxing option to use in an evening bath ritual. Chamomile can also be used to settle nausea and ease irritation from skin conditions such as eczema.

* **Ylang ylang:** often used in perfumes or aromatherapy, thanks to its beautiful fragrance, this oil has calming effects on mood and can assist in lowering both blood pressure and heart rate. A few drops of ylang ylang oil will transform your bath into a calming oasis.

To complete your bath ritual, adorn the room with candles to create a relaxing ambience. You can also add two handfuls of Epsom salt to the water, to help ease muscle pain and tension.

*"Lord, make us mindful of the little things that grow and blossom in these days to make the world beautiful for us."*

– William Edward Burghardt Du Bois –

# Gratitude journaling

Taking a few moments to write down what you are grateful for is a really great way to appreciate life's simple joys. Keeping a regular gratitude journal is a wonderful mood booster and will help protect your wellbeing during stressful times. If you build this practice into your routine, you will experience gratitude at the moment of writing, as well as gain a prolonged sense of appreciation throughout the day, while your journal is held in the back of your mind.

# Gratitude journaling tips

* The act of writing something down brings enhanced focus and helps to create a lasting memory. It's a great idea to keep your journal in a physical notebook, rather than a phone or tablet, as this will deepen your experience.

* Keeping a gratitude journal with a partner or family member is a fantastic way to appreciate things you may not have noticed before, or to recall positive experiences you'd forgotten about. If you both work through the same prompts (see p. 32) and then compare answers, you'll discover a lot to be grateful for.

* If you find yourself stuck for inspiration, remember the little moments: perhaps you spotted a sweet dog on your walk to work, or you noticed the colors of autumn emerging in the trees.

* The easiest way to make a routine for your gratitude diary is to stick with a consistent structure and a regular writing time. For example, you might keep a notebook by your bedside and list "five things you were grateful for today" right before you fall asleep. Simplicity and regularity are the tools that will really ingrain your new habit.

* Our brains organize our memories during sleep, so writing in this journal before bed is a sure way to develop a grateful way of thinking.

# Here are twenty prompts to help you on your way to gratitude journaling:

1. What is something you enjoyed today?
2. What is something you are looking forward to?
3. What is your happiest memory?
4. Who are you grateful to have met in your life, and why?
5. Where is your favorite place?
6. Where do you feel safe?
7. What is your favorite season, and what do you like about it?
8. What personality traits are you glad you have?
9. Which of your recent social interactions are you grateful for?
10. Which friends do you most value?
11. Which musicians are you glad exist?
12. What are your favorite family memories?
13. What do you like about where you live?
14. What is your favorite sound?
15. What is your favorite taste?
16. Describe your favorite pet and what you like about it.
17. When was the last time you laughed, and what made you laugh?
18. Have you ever received a random act of kindness?
19. Have you ever provided a random act of kindness?
20. Describe a time when you felt truly at peace.

Once you've got the hang of these prompts, try thinking of some of your own. You'll realize there is so much to be grateful for.

There are many ways for you to welcome the practice of mindfulness into your life. The key is to find a routine that works for you. A little bit of daily practice will bring long-term relief and resilience to stress. Regular mindfulness allows you to see beauty in the simple things, providing you with a strong foundation to help you endure whatever life throws your way.

# HOME

# HOME

When we think of cottage interiors, we think of an eclectic mix of vintage and antique furniture, a happy clutter where every item has a story to tell. Building materials are often exposed—perhaps a brick wall, a flagstone floor, a stone fireplace surround, or timber ceiling beams. Raw materials are cherished and celebrated, warps in wooden floorboards are welcome, for they allow us to imagine the pottering of feet across the years. Old buildings have stories to tell, and we want them to be told.

The aim of Cottagecore is to recreate the safe and cozy vibe of an old cottage in our homes, regardless of whether our space is old or new. It doesn't have to be a major renovation. A comfy armchair, a vintage floor lamp, and a stack of old books will provide a welcoming reading nook in the corner of a room and can make you feel like you're relaxing in a cabin that's nestled in the woods.

The phrase "one man's trash is another man's treasure" certainly holds true here. For those who are choosing to modernize their homes,

antique and vintage furniture becomes a hindrance in need of removal. With a quick search on Facebook Marketplace, or eBay, you should be able to find some bargains nearby. Bulky items such as armchairs, sofas, and tables can often be found at low prices, where folks are in a hurry to get rid of the old and bring in the new. Using search terms such as "vintage," "antique," "shabby," "Victorian," and "farmhouse," should give you a good place to start when looking online. For the best deals, try second-hand stores, vintage fairs, flea markets, and estate sales.

Beyond saving money, another great reason for buying second-hand is sustainability. When we buy something new, we exploit resources such as wood or cotton, oftentimes via unethical labor practices and habitat destruction. Creating and transporting new goods leaves a large carbon footprint, too, especially when we consider the short lifespan if an item that is thrown away after a few years. By buying second-hand, we both avoid creating something new and prevent something old from going to waste.

You'll also find that vintage items are built to last. These days, items are often designed to break or go out of fashion—this is known as planned obsolescence and it ensures that we keep spending money. The older the item, the better chance it was created with craftsmanship and timeless design in mind; if it has lasted for the better part of a century, you'll likely have many more happy years with it. And if you need any more reasons to shop second-hand, vintage shopping is way more exciting than buying new! Your items will likely be one of a kind and hard to mimic.

"Home is the
nicest word
there is."

– Laura Ingalls Wilder –

# Cottagecore
# interior checklist

Here are some classic Cottagecore furnishings to look for on your hunt
for vintage treasure. Don't worry if you find objects that are a little
worn—it only adds to their charm!

* Needlework cushion covers
* Pine dressers, sideboards, shelves, and farmhouse tables
* Chintz curtains and fabrics
* Voile curtains
* Porcelain ornaments such as Staffordshire dogs
* Fairy lights
* Wooden or brass candlesticks
* Old oil paintings
* Baroque-style picture frames
* Vintage books
* Wicker baskets
* Striped or microprint wallpaper
* Matte, water-based wall paint
* White cotton tablecloths and doilies
* Vintage cutlery
* Mismatched ornaments and memorabilia
* Record players and vinyl

* Dried flowers
* Rocking chairs
* Chandeliers and lanterns
* Oriental rugs
* Vintage floor lamps
* Wool throws and blankets for chairs, sofas, and beds
* Grandfather clocks
* Iron or French-style bedframes
* Antique sofas or chaises
* Armchairs
* Wreaths
* Vintage china such as Blue Willow or Asiatic Pheasant
* Linen or cotton bedspreads, eiderdowns, quilts, ruffled valances, and voile or cotton bed canopies

# Houseplants

A houseplant is an easy way to breathe a bit of Cottagecore into your living space. Houseplants can improve mood and reduce stress. There are plenty to choose from, and many are low maintenance. In the cottage spirit of being both ornamental and purposeful, some houseplants—such as mint or lavender—are useful in the kitchen, too.

## Boston fern

The Boston fern is a plant that was popularized by the Victorians. It's fantastic for bringing some green into your indoor space. This fern is suited to a room with less direct light. As the Boston fern loves humidity, it is especially well suited to a bathroom, but you can keep it happy in most rooms, as long as you water it regularly and mist occasionally.

# Pelargoniums

Pelargoniums, also known as indoor or scented geraniums, are a generously flowering houseplant. They are native to South Africa and became a popular feature of the European country home during the Victorian era. Pelargoniums are easy to look after; they are drought tolerant, so be sure not to overwater them. They love the sun and are not cold hardy. They will do best on a sunny windowsill.

Pelargonium flowers and leaves are edible and richly scented; they make great decorations for salads and cakes. The essential oils found in pelargoniums, which can be purchased, are also said to relieve anxiety and depression, as well as deter insects, such as mosquitoes and wasps.

One of the most appealing things about pelargoniums is the enormous range of colors and sizes available. Whether you love large plants and bright colors or dainty pastel flowers, you can be sure to find a variety to suit your indoor space.

## Lemon tree

If you have the space and light available for a lemon tree, you'll benefit from both its beautiful, evergreen foliage and the occasional lemon harvest. The Meyer variety of lemon tree 10-13 ft (roughly 3-4m) tall, requiring a 10-3 ft (3-4m) space around it, is well suited to indoor growing. If you have a porch or conservatory, or if your place has large windows that get at least eight hours of direct sunlight per day, you can welcome a lemon tree or two into your home. They are a little more work than other houseplants, but you can't beat a lemon drizzle cake made with home-grown lemons!

## Myrtle topiary

Myrtle topiaries are a fantastic way to add a bit of formality and class to your living space. A neatly clipped topiary evokes images of stately homes or the gardens of a French château. The scented leaves of myrtle can also be used in cooking, making it a multifunctional houseplant. Myrtle plants require full sun, so they are perfect for conservatories, porches, and balconies. They also like cold conditions and grow best at a distance from central heating.

# Herbs

An indoor herb garden brings the perfect mix of beauty and functionality. Many herb varieties are rooted in cottage history, thanks to their medicinal properties and culinary uses. Herb gardens can also be incredibly economical—you can grow herbs in tin cans, as long as you've cut a small drainage hole at the bottom. Many herbs—such as mint, rosemary and thyme—will root from cuttings: after you've bought a packet of fresh herbs from the supermarket, place three or four 4-6 in (10-15 cm) lengths in a cup of water, ideally on an indirectly-lit windowsill. After a week or so, you should see tiny white roots appearing from the submerged part of the plant. When you notice your cutting has rooted, go ahead and plant it in a small container of potting soil, and soon enough you will have a selection of free plants!

Perennial herbs such as mint, rosemary, thyme, and oregano don't need to be regrown every year, so they are great, low-maintenance options. As long as you're not too greedy with picking from them, they should grow happily over the long term. Herbs such as parsley, basil, and cilantro have a shorter lifespan and will need to be replaced after a few harvests, but they are easy to grow from seed.

# Ivy

There's nothing like an ivy plant to evoke a fairy-tale image. Ivies are known as prolific growers in the garden, but by containing them in a pot, you'll have a rewarding houseplant that grows quickly without overtaking your space. Ivy plants need a decent amount of natural or artificial light—a windowsill with indirect sunlight is perfect. If you get a lot of light throughout your room, they look enchanting trailing across a bookshelf.

# Cut flowers

Cut flowers are a cottage staple. Vintage milk jugs or stoneware pots make great vases. For smaller bunches, an old jelly jar will do just fine. If you don't grow flowers at home, you may want to pick up a bunch from your supermarket or greengrocer. Alternatively, you can look for foraged blooms, such as daisies, cow parsley, or Queen Anne's Lace.

# Photographing interiors

Once you're satisfied that your interior has captured Cottagecore charm, it's time to share the magic on social media. Whether you're using your smartphone or professional camera gear for interior photography, there are a few things you can do to really bring the space to life.

The first and most important rule is to pay attention to the light in a room. Unless you are going for an evening glow, natural and diffused daylight will do the best job at highlighting your space, and you should try to keep artificial lights switched off. Experiment with pulling back curtains or blinds to get as much natural light into the space as possible. Adding mirrors and reflective surfaces to dark corners will help to soften shadows. If your room is in direct sunlight, you may struggle at midday when the sun is at its highest point—shooting at this time can result in strong shadows that make details hard to see. Instead, try early in the morning, late afternoon, or a cloudy day. Because all rooms are different, it's important to pay attention to light changes throughout the day to find the time that works best for your space.

Before photographing, it's worth tidying up a bit. To complete the vintage feel, you may want to hide modern appliances such as TVs or games consoles (unless there is a way to seamlessly integrate them into your space). Tuck away exposed wires and hide smaller bits of clutter, such as laptops and magazines. There is an acceptable amount of clutter within the Cottagecore vibe though, so a simple tidying up should suffice.

Don't be afraid to play around with layout. In a living room, you might have sofas and chairs set up for optimal television watching, and that's fine, but it may not be optimal for photography. Take a few photos using the original layout, move things around a bit and then take another photo and compare. Keep playing around until you find an arrangement that photographs well.

From a technical perspective, bear in mind the following:

* It is often best to shoot interiors dead on—perhaps best popularized as the Wes Anderson angle. You want to stand directly opposite your subject and hold your camera at around chest height. Try to capture some symmetry, straight lines, or balance within the frame, as this will appear pleasing to the eye.

* If you find yourself in a smaller space, you can try using a wide-angle lens, or wide setting on your phone, if that's an option. This will showcase as much of your space as possible. Failing that, don't be afraid of photographing details and close-ups.

* Cottages are typically small, dark, and pokey spaces—by nature, they are really difficult to photograph. It can be very rewarding to spend some time styling a little cozy scene—perhaps a cup of tea and an open book

on the edge of an armchair. You'll be surprised by how few details are needed to create a welcoming, rustic mood in a photo.

* The easiest way to edit your photos is through apps. The VSCO app provides a selection of filters based on analogue film. You can also use the grain, vignette, and fade tools to emulate vintage photography. Another popular editing tool is Snapseed—best for editing specific parts of your photos; for example, you can use the brush tool to increase exposure in poorly lit areas.

Overall, when it comes to taking photos, every shot has value. If you shoot your space and it doesn't look right, it's a lesson learned. Spend some time experimenting until you find a way to capture that magical Cottagecore mood. Every great photographer started somewhere, so try to enjoy the journey!

Cottagecore interiors are playful, busy, and happily cluttered. There is plenty of space to experiment and show off your personality. Before mass production, cottage dwellers would often stencil or hand-paint their walls, floors, and shelves, and imperfections only added to the personality of the space. The more vintage items the better, though modern comforts are always a welcome addition. It's time to go thrifting, play around and, most importantly, have fun in the process.

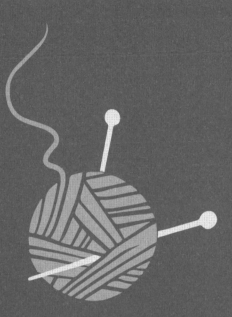

# FASHION

# FASHION

Cottagecore fashion looks at the past through rose-tinted glasses. Through linen pinafores, floral microprints, and floaty dresses we might imagine ourselves as characters from *Pride and Prejudice* or *Wuthering Heights*. Dressing up with historical reference allows us to feel as though we are part of a classic novel, yet we write our own narrative and are not bound by former societal values.

There is a playfulness within Cottagecore fashion that allows you to truly express your identity. You can accessorize your Victorian-inspired frock with custom embroidery or embellishments—perhaps color your hair brightly or adorn yourself with winged eyeliner and tattoos. Outfits that were traditionally assigned as either masculine or feminine can be combined or switched. Cottagecore style can be an artform that showcases the spectrum of gender expression.

Just adding small elements of Cottagecore fashion can bring a comforting touch to your everyday outfit. A simple vintage accessory goes a long way.

# Vintage outfit basics

There is lots of room to experiment with Cottagecore fashion. Here are some styles to get you started.

## Regency dress

If you've watched adaptations of *Pride and Prejudice*, then you will have seen a selection of Regency dresses, from the simple figure-highlighting day dress to the more extravagant ballroom affair. These dresses don't look out of place if you're visiting a stately home, formal garden, or a nice hotel, and if you'd like to style some Cottagecore photos for your Instagram account, even better.

Features of Regency-style dresses include empire waistlines, a square or low neckline, and small puffed sleeves. For formal use, these would have been "dressed up" with silk gloves, pearl necklaces, and waist ribbons. But without any of these accessories they are versatile dresses that can be worn during the day, particularly if they are neutral in color and made of natural fabric. A Regency dress is the perfect way to add some Elizabeth Bennet vibes to your wardrobe.

## Prairie dress

The prairie dress is probably the style you'll see the most while browsing the Cottagecore hashtag on Instagram. If you've watched an adaptation of *Little Women*, you will recognize this style, characterized by high necklines, long sleeves, and a full skirt, and often adorned with ruffles and frills. You can find prairie dresses made of light cotton for summer or a heavier cord material, which is perfect for keeping warm in autumn, paired with tights and boots.

## Smock

A smock is a relaxed-fit dress that tapers out from the neckline. There are plenty of modern smocks available, but occasionally you will find a vintage-style that captures the Cottagecore aesthetic. Look for high or Peter Pan collars, long or puffed sleeves, linen, light cotton or cord material, and a floral, plain, or microprint pattern. Pockets are always a bonus!

## Pinafore and blouse

A pinafore is a full and sleeveless apron, often with buttons or a means of fastening at the back. It is a classic Cottagecore wardrobe staple. Paired with a linen or cotton ruffled blouse in a neutral color, the pinafore is comfortable, practical, and attractive. Look for linen or woollen pinafores, again in neutral colors, to create a historic cottager-style outfit, or cord/denim ones for a more modern adaptation.

# Linens

Linen skirts, blouses, and frocks are often available new. They are extremely comfortable and have great temperature regulation for hot summer days. Look for neutral colors and skirt designs with plenty of long, floaty fabric. Thanks to their light weight, linen dresses and skirts can be great for Cottagecore-styled Instagram shots: just give the skirt a swoosh and run slowly into the woods for perfect fairy-tale vibes every time.

# Cloaks

Dressing to suit the Cottagecore style is much easier in warm temperatures, where just a long, cool dress will do. As the temperature drops and we need to wear more layers, it can be harder to recreate that fairy-tale mood. Cloaks are great for bridging this gap. A shorter cloak that's similar to a poncho is quite easy to style into a modern outfit. And a long cloak with a large hood works fabulously if you're going all out with the fantasy image.

# Dungarees

A good pair of jeans will see you through the practical side of a Cottagecore life, particularly if you're interested in outdoor activities. Jeans can be accessorised with long, lace-up boots, a frilly blouse and a vintage locket to bring in a touch of historic influence without going full-blown cottager. In colder weather, pair jeans with a heavy wool sweater for the ultimate in cozy comfort.

# Cords and tweed

Having a few cord or tweed items in your wardrobe is another way to get through the colder months without compromising on your country-inspired look. A pair of high-waisted cord pants teamed with a shirt and waistcoat makes for a winter outfit that's perfect for walking or gardening.

# Blouse and jeans

A good, ruffled blouse can be teamed with jeans or shorts for a modern Cottagecore twist. If you're out in public and you don't want to commit to a full Victorian smock, a vintage Edwardian-style blouse should do the trick.

# Cottagecore accessory box

Accumulating a few of the following items allows you to either add a subtle hint of vintage to an everyday outfit or to complete a full prairie-inspired costume.

* Straw hat
* Silk handkerchief
* Vintage watch or pocket watch
* Vintage leather belt and gloves
* Tweed hat
* High lace-up boots
* Frilled socks
* Tartan or ribbed socks
* Vintage locket
* Vintage brooch

* Vintage glasses
* Tweed or tartan tie/bowtie
* Woven straw handbag or basket
* Floral choker necklace
* Floral earrings
* Pearl necklace or headband
* Flower crown
* Hair ribbons
* Embroidered clothing

"Simplicity is the ultimate sophistication."

– Leonardo da Vinci –

# Sourcing your Cottagecore look

Thanks to the Victoriana revival of the 1960s–70s, historically inspired clothing isn't too difficult to source second-hand. Many vintage Victorian or Regency-style dresses are actually less than sixty years old, so they are still in relatively good condition compared to their antique and original counterparts. Particularly in the 1960s, these country-inspired dresses, skirts and blouses were extremely well made, crafted from heavy cotton, linen, or other natural fibers. Laura Ashley, a pioneer of the Victorian fashion revival, took print inspiration from wallpapers in the National Trust archives and other historic collections. She developed a romantic style of dress that was a breath of fresh air among modern styles.

# Sourcing vintage clothes online

Online, you can source vintage outfits through eBay, Depop, Facebook Marketplace, and occasionally Instagram, if you follow vintage sellers. If you are buying from a vintage shop that has a curated style, you can expect a higher price tag. If you know what to look for on eBay or Facebook Marketplace, you'll have a better chance of finding a bargain from someone who is clearing out an old wardrobe.

As the Cottagecore movement has gained popularity, modern designers and small businesses have started making country-style dresses and linens, too. For authentic styles, look for small businesses on Etsy that specialize in clothing for re-enactments. A search for "custom prairie dress" should yield some small designers. Buying dresses this way gives you control over sizes, cuts, collars, sleeve style, and fabric choice, so you can choose dresses that are unique to you. It's also surprisingly inexpensive when compared to some of the designer Cottagecore styles.

Use the following search terms to track down vintage treasures online:

* Vintage
* Retro
* Prairie dress
* Linen
* Cotton
* Cottagecore
* 60s

* 70s
* 80s
* Regency
* Victorian
* Edwardian
* Gunne Sax
* Laura Ashley

# Vintage shopping offline

Offline, you can source vintage outfits through second-hand or thrift shops, flea markets, vintage fairs, vintage stores, and garage sales. This method takes a bit more labor, but you are more likely to find a bargain, particularly if you shop at thrift stores.

Cottagecore has started to find its way into "fast fashion," though these designs are often poorly and unethically made, not created to last, and have prints that are not quite as charming. If the option of buying second-hand or vintage is available to you, it's the most rewarding and sustainable route.

# Photographing Cottagecore fashion

* **As with many areas of photography, natural light is your best friend.**
  Try early-morning mist or the golden hour (before sunset) for an
  extra layer of atmosphere.

* **If you don't have someone to help shoot your outfit for you, you can
  use a tripod and the timer setting on your phone or camera to set up
  your own shots.** It takes a little bit of practice to master posing and
  composition, but it is well worth the effort.

* **The key to photographing Cottagecore fashion is styling.** The easiest
  and most effective hack is to wear a skirt or dress that has plenty of
  fabric, and that flows well when "swooshed."

* **Pick a setting that complements the country outfit**—say, under a tree,
  in a field, or sit at a vintage table.

* **Style your scene further with props,** such as a picnic blanket, vintage
  book or parasol.

* **Poses that don't connect directly with the camera can help to create a
  photo that's reminiscent of a vintage painting.** Try walking away from
  the camera, looking at something in the distance, or engaging with a
  pet or a prop.

* **Edit your photos with a vintage-film-inspired filter;** the VSCO app is
  perfect for this (see p. 53)

Cottagecore fashion can be as minimal or as eccentric as you wish. It's a means of self-expression; by playing with your image you can play with your story, or simply add a little touch of nostalgia. If you have the option, searching vintage and second-hand shops for treasure can be incredibly fulfilling and your outfits will be one of a kind.

# GARDENING

# GARDENING

When you fall in love with gardening, you will always have something to look forward to on the horizon. Even in the depths of winter, you can plant a pot of tulip bulbs and watch every day as they build momentum towards their spring display. Gardening inspires connection among people and protection of the natural world: communities can come together to develop neighborhood gardens or maintain or protect an undeveloped patch of land; you can exchange seeds or cut flowers with your next-door neighbor; or perhaps write to your community council and point out a green belt that could benefit from some trees or wildflower seeds.

Land ownership is not a prerequisite to feeling the joys of a garden. Plenty of plants and vegetables can be grown in pots on patios, balconies, and windowsills—even on your dining-room table. Thankfully, many private gardens are open to visitors and can be found online. So if you don't take part in the gardening process yourself, you can still enjoy observing seasonal change in your spare time.

There are a number of reasons why you might want to garden. The health benefits are extremely well documented. From physical exercise and exposure to vitamin D to the release of mood-boosting endorphins, it's hard to find a reason why not to give it a go. If you are growing your own herbs or vegetables, these can make for nutrient-rich seasonal meals. They taste great, they're healthy, and unlike imported produce, they don't rack up air miles.

You might also want to garden to benefit nature. As our insect population continues to decline, it becomes increasingly vital for us to plant habitats and food sources to offer them some protection. By welcoming smaller creatures, we also welcome biodiversity through the rest of the food chain. If we let snails into the garden, frogs might be partial to snacking on them. The frogs will attract birds, and the birds, in turn, attract foxes. As if by magic, there is a restored ecosystem at play, stemming from just a few plants. Finally, there is the soil. Our soil is the foundation of plant, animal, and human health, and it is vital we take care of it. As plants decompose, they transfer carbon from the atmosphere into the soil, creating a "carbon sink," whereby the carbon acts as food for the soil's ecosystems. With the right methods, we can use soil health to capture carbon and help us fight climate change.

"That is one good thing about this world . . . there are always sure to be more springs."

– L. M. Montgomery –

# Growing cottage flowers

When designing a cottage garden, window box, or arrangement of pots, the key is to have something flowering in every season. This means there will always be a focal point, and your space will never look bare. The most challenging times are autumn and winter, when many trees and hedges shed their leaves, and few plants are in flower. There is still, however, a surprisingly large selection that blooms through this period to carry your display through. In bigger spaces, you can also use evergreen hedges, such as box and yew, to provide a backdrop through winter.

There are a few basics to get familiar with before we get started, but don't worry too much about learning all of the technicalities now. The easiest way to learn is by giving it a try.

Your flower display can be built from perennials, biennials, annuals, and bulbs. If you are working in a patio or a garden, you may also want to add shrubs, hedges, and trees to create structure.

# Flower meanings

You might be familiar with sending red roses on Valentine's day as a gesture of love, but they are not the only flowers that have a deep meaning. There are flowers that symbolize everything from love and passion to ambition and happiness—in fact, there is an entire language of flowers, known as floriography, and it is as rich as the human experience itself. Here are the meanings associated with some cottage favorites that you might like to add to your garden:

**Calla lily (white)**—purity and innocence

**Daffodil (just one)**—rebirth and new beginnings

**Daffodils (a bunch)**—joy and happiness

**Gladiolus**—remembrance

**Hollyhock**—ambition

**Iris (purple)**—compliments and wisdom

**Iris (yellow)**—passion

**Iris (white)**—purity

**Lilac**—youthful innocence

**Mint**—virtue

**Rose (red)**—love

**Salvia (red)**—forever mine

**Snapdragon**—deception

**Tulip (red)**—passion

# Perennials

These are plants that flower every year, and as such, they can be a reliable confidence boost if you are new to gardening. Often, they will get bigger over time, and after a few years of growing perennials, you may be able to divide the plants, so you gain more for free. Perennials are usually herbaceous, which means the stems die back in the winter, but the roots will remain underground ready for the next growing season. Popular cottage perennials include delphiniums, peonies, and catmint.

# Biennials

Biennials are plants with a two-year lifecycle. In their first year, they will establish a basic structure of roots, stems, and leaves. Then, they will flower in their second year, after which they will drop seeds. To maintain a yearly display of flowering biennials, you will need to add plants every year in preparation for flowering in the year to come. Popular cottage-garden biennials include foxgloves and hollyhocks.

## Annuals

Annuals will flower and set seed within one year. Though the original plant won't return the following year, it will likely drop plenty of seeds that will give you new plants. You can use annuals to fill in the gaps in your display, or you could create a cut-flower area from them. Well-known cottage garden annuals include cosmos, poppies, and cornflowers—all of which make great cut-flower displays to bring into your home.

## Bulbs

A bulb is a plant that stores its life cycle in a layered, underground structure. Bulbs are usually perennial plants (they flower every year in the right conditions) and are either spring or summer–autumn flowering. Common cottage-garden blubs include tulips and daffodils (spring flowering) and gladioli and oriental lilies (autumn flowering).

## Shrubs

A shrub is a long-lasting plant with woody stems. Some shrubs are evergreen, while others lose their leaves over winter. Because of their rigid shape, shrubs are a good way to lend structure to your garden, and many flower generously, too. Cottage favorites include butterfly bush, lilac, and roses.

"To plant a garden is to believe in tomorrow."

– Audrey Hepburn –

# Growing vegetables

Cottage gardens are typically a mix of productive and ornamental plants. Not only does this look beautiful it also encourages biodiversity within your growing space, as flowers will bring in pollinators, and these, in turn, will pollinate your produce. Everybody wins!

Many vegetables are grown as annuals, so they produce food within the year they are planted and are then cleared away and composted. There are also perennial plants that give us a harvest every year, making them low maintenance and high reward. It's worth introducing a few of these into your space, so you will always have something to harvest.

## Perennial crops for a low-maintenance vegetable garden

* Rhubarb
* Asparagus
* Jerusalem artichokes
* Globe artichokes
* Spinach

* Strawberries
* Summer and autumn raspberries
* Blueberries

# Cottage-garden calendar

The following cottage-garden calendar will help guide you through the year. Of course, different locations have differing climates, so if you have mild winters in your area, for example, you may not need to lift tender plants in the autumn. It's worth looking into your garden "zone" and its climate, as this will help you make specific growing choices.

# Spring

Spring is a generous and exciting season in the garden, as life begins to emerge after a winter of rest. Your space may be blessed with blossoming fruit trees—tulips and daffodils will be in flower, and it's the time to sow seeds for annual flowers and vegetables. It's the season of planning your garden year and getting into action.

## Jobs for spring

* **Sow hardy annuals** (to flower this year) including baby's breath, sunflowers, sweet peas, cornflowers, poppies, and night stocks. Hardy annuals can be sown directly into their flowering position in pots or beds, or they can be started in seed trays and transplanted as young plants.

* **Sow half-hardy annuals** (to flower this year) in a greenhouse or on a windowsill, including cosmos, zinnias, marigolds, nasturtiums, and morning glory. These can be planted after the last frost.

* **Harvest remaining crops** that were grown over winter, such as parsnips, sprouts, and spring cabbage.

* **Sow tender vegetable seeds in seed trays,** including chilli, zucchini, squash, pumpkin, tomato, leek, and eggplant. These will need to be kept in a greenhouse or on a windowsill until the frost risk has passed.

* **Sow hardy vegetable seeds directly into beds** or containers, including beets, carrot, pea, radish, spinach, chard, and turnip.

* **Plant** potatoes, onion sets (immature bulbs—easier to grow from than seeds), shallots, and garlic.

* In late spring, your tender and half-hardy sowings can be planted.

## What's in flower now?

Camellia * daffodils * tulips * bluebells * primroses * laburnum * irises * lilac * peonies * wisteria

# Summer

Summer is when cottage-garden displays are usually at their peak. Blooms are abundant, pollinators are well fed, and vases around the house are overflowing with cut flowers. Growth in the garden is at its fastest in summer, and many fruits and vegetables are ready to harvest. Be sure to take the time to admire your growing space while it is at its best.

## *Jobs for summer*

* **Plant dahlia tubers** and autumn-flowering bulbs outdoors, in pots or beds where they are intended to grow.

* **Keep on top of weeding and watering.**

* **Deadhead spent blooms** or cut flowers for vases indoors; this will allow your plants to flower again (deadheading methods vary according to plant type, so it's best to check first how to do this).

* **Support large plants** that are at risk of falling over with wire frames or bamboo canes.

* **Sow perennial seeds**, including columbine, delphinium, and lupin.

* **Sow vegetable seeds** directly into their growing location, including carrot, cauliflower, broccoli, spinach, and radish.

* **Harvest fruits**, including early apples, berries, plums, figs, and peaches.

* **Harvest vegetables**, including eggplant, tomatoes, beets, beans, zucchini, and many more.

## *What's in flower now?*

Delphiniums * peonies * foxgloves * azaleas * freesias * wildflowers * lavender * poppies * roses * sunflowers * dahlias * cosmos * catmint

## Autumn

By autumn, the pace of growth in the garden has slowed down. Many trees are taken over with warm colors before they drop their leaves, and you can harvest hearty vegetables such as squash and pumpkin. While you are putting parts of your growing space to bed, you can begin to plan your spring bulb collections, planting daffodils and tulips to give yourself something to look forward to next year.

## *Jobs for autumn*

* **Plant winter/spring bulbs**, such as daffodils, tulips, crocuses, and snowdrops.

* **Protect tender plants** from frost by bringing them inside, mulching, or storing in a greenhouse.

* **After the first frost, cut away the foliage from dahlia plants.** Lift and rinse the tubers, and then leave them to dry for a few days. Once the tubers are dry, store them in a cardboard box of sawdust or compost in an unheated space such as a shed or garage.

* **Lift gladiolus bulbs with a trowel.** Be careful to leave the foliage attached, as this will feed the bulb. Wipe away any soil, then let the bulbs dry for a few days before storing them for the winter in an empty cardboard box.

* **Collect and compost fallen leaves.**

* **Harvest autumn produce**, including squash, pumpkin, carrots, and autumn raspberries.

* **Sow seeds for growing next spring**, including sweet pea, spring cabbage, onion, and garlic. Note that some varieties will need protection from frost.

## *What's in flower now?*

Dahlias * sunflowers * Japanese anemones * cosmos * marigolds * autumn ox-eye daisies

# Winter

Winter is a time of rest for many plants. Contrary to what you may believe, though, there are still jobs to do in a winter growing space. While lots of plants are dormant, spaces are more accessible, making winter the perfect time to work on construction jobs, such as fixing your shed, building new raised beds, or arranging a new collection of pots. There is also an assortment of winter vegetables to harvest. If you're lucky, you might have a home-grown Christmas dinner.

## *Jobs for winter*

* If you missed out in autumn, **you can still plant your tulip bulbs** at the start of winter.
* **Work on construction jobs** and keep the garden tidy.
* **Harvest winter produce** such as chard, kale, cabbage, broccoli, and Brussels sprouts.
* **There are still a few seeds you may wish to sow,** including winter greens, dill, parsley, and fava beans.

## *What's in flower now?*

Winter clematis * winter jasmine * cyclamen * snowdrops * hellebores * crocuses * camellia * hyacinths

# Upcycling in the garden

Accessorizing your garden doesn't have to be expensive, as there are plenty of quirky ways to upcycle things that would otherwise go to waste. This is eco-friendly and means your growing space will be original and unique.

## Upcycled mini pond

You don't need a lot of space to create a pond for frogs or newts. If you can get your hands on a second-hand farmhouse sink, half whiskey barrel or a small, galvanized trough, it should do the trick. Make sure to plug any holes and then leave your pond outside to collect rainwater (which is more wildlife friendly than tap water). Oxygenating plants, such as hornwort and curly-leaf pondweed, will help to keep the water clear and algae-free, while aquatic flowers, such as water lilies and irises, can make your pond more ornamental. If you have a small pond, aim to place it in the shade, so the water doesn't evaporate in hot weather.

## Bug hotel

You'll often see bug hotels (habitats for insects, particularly during hibernation) for sale in shops and garden centers—and they can be quite expensive. But most of what our insects need for a healthy hibernation exists in our gardens already. If you have some old pallets, it's even easier: stack a few of these on top of one another, or secure four pieces of wood together to create a thick frame. Then fill the gaps with dead wood, twigs, dry leaves, dry sticks, and corrugated cardboard and place your "hotel" somewhere it can sit undisturbed. The more bug hotels you have in your garden, the more you are doing to help protect valuable insect populations.

## Pallet frame for climbers

If you want to grow climbing plants, such as pumpkin and squash, the best way to save space is by growing them vertically. Simply balance two pallets in an inverted V shape, secure them together with string or wire, and your climbing plants will have a frame to grow on.

# Beginners' gardening tips

* **Start with a couple of plants or vegetables that you absolutely love**—this will keep you motivated. Supplement these with a few plants that are easy to grow and highly rewarding, such as roses or radishes. They will give you a feeling of success.

* **Don't be afraid of failure**; some things will go wrong, but that's how we learn! There is still value in a lesson learned.

* **Similarly, nature has its own plan**—we can't always control it, but that can be a blessing. You may have some cottage-garden favorites that self-seed freely all over the garden.

* **Even the most proficient gardeners still feel they have more to learn,** so try not to get too wrapped up in the big picture. There is an immense amount of joy in the smallest of flowers—try to focus on these details if you feel overwhelmed.

* **If you are growing plants, try to avoid growing the same ones in the same container two seasons in a row.** Crop rotation helps to prevent the soil from becoming depleted of specific nutrients or riddled with disease.

* **Avoid pesticides**, as they are harmful to natural and human health. Instead, aim to nurture a natural predatory cycle in the garden or growing space. If you discover aphids on your plants, don't spray

them with pesticide. Leave them be; eventually, ladybugs will be attracted to the plant and will happily snack on the aphids. You could also plant a decoy plant, such as nasturtium or marigold. These are loved by aphids and will encourage predatory ladybugs to control the aphid population.

* **Neem oil** is another useful, natural pest deterrent to look into.

* **Frogs and newts are a great slug control**. Try introducing a pond or a small container of water to encourage frogs and newts into the space (see p. 94).

* **Look into companion planting** as another natural pest deterrent. For example, basil is a successful deterrent to whiteflies and is often planted near tomatoes to prevent infestation.

* **Many plants will grow happily in pots.** Be sure to keep them watered in hot weather and use a good-quality, peat-free compost to give them nutrients.

It might seem there is a lot to learn in the garden, but the hardest part is getting started. Once you get going and feel your hands in the soil, relaxation and enjoyment will take over, and you'll soon think there's nothing to worry about. There is as much joy in the process as there is in the end result (maybe even more). However big or small your growing project, let it bring you plenty of contentment.

# FOOD

# FOOD:
# EATING AND COOKING
# WITH THE SEASONS

Historically, cottagers would have eaten seasonally as part of their way of
life. Produce would have been grown in a nearby plot, harvested fresh,
and then prepared over the fireplace. Though we might not have the
means to be self-sufficient today, we know there are plenty of reasons
to eat seasonal, local produce: you may want to take better care of your
health, reduce food waste, or adopt a more climate- and environment-
friendly diet. Or maybe you simply want to enjoy the taste of fresh
ingredients.

# How to shop seasonally

Many of us are interested in adopting a more seasonal eating pattern, but don't have the means to grow our own food, or at least not in a large enough quantity to be self-sufficient. Thankfully, there are a few things you can try to make the most of your local food supply.

To start, it helps to learn a little bit about what produce is in season throughout the year. This will give you an awareness of what to look for while you are shopping. If you want to make sure you're supporting local producers in particular, it's worth looking into foods that are grown in your specific climate, month by month, as seasonal produce can vary significantly around the world. Here is a quick guide based on temperate growing conditions.

# Spring

Arugula * Asparagus * Beets * Cabbage * Elderflower * Fava beans * Green onions (scallions) * Leeks * New potatoes * Peas * Purple sprouting broccoli * Radishes * Rhubarb * Spring greens * Watercress

# Summer

Apples * Asparagus * Beets * Blackcurrants * Blueberries * Broccoli * Carrots * Cherries * Cucumbers * Eggplant * Elderflower * Fava beans * Fennel * French beans * Globe artichokes * Gooseberries * Loganberries * Mushrooms * Pears * Peas * Plums * Radishes * Redcurrants * Rhubarb * Runner beans * Shallots * Strawberries * Sweetcorn * Tomatoes * Turnips * Zucchini

# Autumn

Apples * Broccoli * Brussels sprouts * Cauliflower * Celeriac * Chicory * Crab apples * Jerusalem artichokes * Kale * Parsnips * Pears * Plums * Pumpkin * Quinces * Rutabaga * Sloes * Squash * Turnips * Wild mushrooms

# Winter

Apples * Cabbage * Carrots * Celeriac * Celery * Forced rhubarb * Jerusalem artichokes * Kale * Leeks * Parsnips * Pears * Pumpkin * Purple sprouting broccoli * Rutabaga * Turnips

If you live in a city or only have a supermarket nearby, be sure to check where the produce is grown. If it matches the country you live in, you'll know the produce is currently in season. It might take a little bit of time to get the hang of this, but you'll soon develop a habit, based on a rough idea of what to shop for during each season.

In the city, you may also have access to zero-waste markets for grains, flours, legumes, and more. Many of these items store well, so buying them in a particular season isn't necessarily important. However, stores that stock zero-waste produce will often source their products from ethical suppliers around the world to ensure their growers are paid fairly. There is plenty of value in that if you have the means to support your nearest zero-waste market.

If you live in a more rural setting, look for nearby farm stands and markets, where you should be able to source local and seasonal produce. You may also have a greengrocer nearby. It's worth having a look around to assess the options. Note that you may still need to pay attention to the growing location of your produce, as some farm stores and greengrocers may import out-of-season items.

"One cannot think
well, love well, sleep
well, if one has
not dined well."

– Virginia Woolf –

# Seasonal recipe ideas

Each season presents us with ingredients we can really celebrate.
Whether it's a light rhubarb crumble in the spring or a hearty vegetable
soup in the winter, there's something incredibly comforting about a meal
made of fresh, local produce.

# *Spring*

# Rhubarb Peanut Crumble

Spring is rhubarb season, and what better way to celebrate than with a classic rhubarb crumble with a peanut twist? It's sweet and tangy, with a creamy and crunchy topping.

*Serves 4 · Prep 15 minutes · Cooking time 20–25 minutes*

Butter, for greasing

2 lb 4 oz/8 cups (1 kg) rhubarb, sliced

2 oz/¼ cup (50 g) superfine sugar

2 tbsp cold water

1 tsp ground cinnamon

Cream, crème fraîche, ice cream, or custard, to serve

**For the peanut-butter crumble:**

4 oz/1 cup (100 g) all-purpose flour

2 oz/½ cup (50 g) old-fashioned oats (rolled oats)

2 oz/¼ cup (50 g) light brown or turbinado sugar

3 oz/generous ¼ cup (75 g) crunchy peanut butter

2 oz/¼ cup (50 g) butter, diced

1. Preheat the oven to 375°F (190°C/170°C fan/gas 5). Lightly butter a shallow ovenproof baking dish.

2. Make the peanut-butter crumble: mix together the flour, oats, and sugar in a large mixing bowl. Break the peanut butter into lumps and add them to the bowl with the diced butter. Using your fingertips, rub in the two butters until the mixture resembles fine breadcrumbs.

*…recipe continued overleaf*

3. Mix the rhubarb, sugar, and water in a bowl. Sprinkle with the cinnamon, and then pour the mixture into the buttered baking dish.

4. Sprinkle the crumble mixture evenly over the rhubarb, levelling the top, so the fruit is completely covered. Bake in the preheated oven for 20–25 minutes until the topping is crisp and golden brown and the filling is cooked and tender.

5. Serve warm with cream, crème fraîche, ice cream, or custard. This also tastes good eaten cold the following day.

## Variations

* *Make the crumble at other times of the year, using whatever fruit is in season—pears, apples, cherries, blackberries, green or black plums, apricots, or even strawberries.*

# *Summer*

# Basil Pesto

Basil plants thrive in the summer, and this pesto recipe
is a quick and easy way to make the most of your harvest.
Serve it with pasta for a simple, seasonal lunch.

*Serves 4 · Prep 5 minutes*

2 oz/⅓ cup (50 g) pine nuts, toasted
½ garlic clove
½ oz/¾ cup (15 g) fresh basil, leaves picked
4 oz/just under ½ cup (100 ml) olive oil
Sea salt flakes
Freshly ground black pepper

1. Using a pestle and mortar, lightly crush the pine nuts until they begin to break down. Add the garlic to the mortar and crush again. Next, add the basil and half of the olive oil, and continue to crush until the basil softens. You are looking for the leaves to break down and release their natural oils, but not quite so much that they begin to turn brown.

2. Transfer the contents of the mortar to a bowl and whisk in the rest of the oil, along with a generous pinch of salt and black pepper. Taste, and adjust the seasoning if needed.

## *Autumn*

# Roasted Beets

An autumn harvest isn't complete without a good supply of beets. Here is a simple dish that can be served as a light lunch or a side. If you don't have black mustard seeds, use brown mustard seed—about 1½ times the amount of black mustard seeds specified in the recipe.

*Serves 4 · Prep 5 minutes · Cooking time 30–40 minutes*

1 lb raw beets (450 g), peeled and cut into wedges (about 3⅓ cups)
2 tbsp olive oil
1 tsp black mustard seeds
Balsamic vinegar, for drizzling (optional)
Sea salt

1. Preheat the oven to 425°F (220°C/200°C fan/gas 7).

2. Toss the beet wedges with the oil and mustard seeds in a large bowl. Place them in a roasting pan and sprinkle with a pinch of sea salt. Roast in the preheated oven for 30–40 minutes, until tender. Drizzle with balsamic vinegar (if using) before serving.

# *Winter*

# Creamy Brussels Sprouts Soup With Cheesy Croûtes

Brussels sprouts are often divisive—they seem to be a love/
hate thing for many people. However, if you source fresh, in-
season sprouts, you'll find it hard not to enjoy the flavor. Here is
a comforting soup recipe to make the most of your harvest.

*Serves 4 • Prep 15 minutes • Cooking time 35–40 minutes*

2 tbsp olive oil

1 large onion, chopped

2 garlic cloves, crushed

10 oz (300 g) celeriac, peeled
and diced (about 2 cups)

14 oz/3½ cups (400 g) Brussels
sprouts, trimmed and halved

1 litre (4 cups) vegetable stock

4 sprigs of thyme, leaves stripped

4 oz/½ cup (120 ml)
crème fraîche

Sea salt and freshly
ground black pepper

For the cheesy croûtes:

4 thin slices baguette,
cut diagonally

2 tsp Dijon mustard

3½ oz/1 cup (100 g) grated
Cheddar cheese

1. Heat the olive oil in a large saucepan over low heat and cook the onion and garlic, stirring occasionally, for 8–10 minutes until softened but not browned. Add the celeriac and cook gently for 2 minutes.

2. Stir in the sprouts and cook for 5 minutes. Add the stock and thyme leaves and bring to a boil. Reduce the heat to a gentle simmer and cook for 15–20 minutes, or until the vegetables are really tender.

3. Process the soup in a blender until smooth—you can do this in batches. Transfer the soup to the pan and season to taste with salt and pepper. Stir in the crème fraîche and reheat gently.

4. Meanwhile, make the cheesy croûtes: lightly toast the baguette slices under the broiler. Spread each slice with a thin layer of mustard.

5. Pour the soup into 4 heatproof bowls and float the baguette slices, mustard-side up, on top. Sprinkle the soup with the grated cheese and pop the bowls under the broiler just long enough to melt the cheese. Serve immediately.

## Variations

* *Top with crumbled crispy bacon or pancetta for a non-vegetarian version.*
* *Use a large potato and 2 celery stalks instead of the celeriac.*

"Good food is
the foundation
of genuine
happiness."

– Auguste Escoffier –

# Baking

## Herby Halloumi Scones

The humble scone is a cottage classic. This savory recipe
uses herbs and halloumi for a perfect lunchtime treat.

*Makes 6 scones • Prep 15 minutes • Cooking time 10—15 minutes*

8 oz/1¾ cups (225 g)
self-rising flour, plus
extra for dusting

1½ tsp baking powder

½ tsp salt

½ tsp mustard powder

2 oz/¼ cup (50 g) butter,
diced, plus extra for greasing

1 tbsp black (or brown)
mustard seeds
A few sprigs of mint,
finely chopped

4 oz/1 cup (125 g)
grated halloumi, plus
extra for sprinkling

1 medium free-range
egg, beaten

3–4 oz/⅓ cup (90–100 ml)
milk, plus extra for brushing

2 tbsp sesame seeds

Cayenne pepper, for dusting

1. Preheat the oven to 425°F (220°C/200°C fan/gas 7). Lightly butter a
cookie sheet.

2. Sift the flour and baking powder into a large mixing bowl. Mix in the salt
and mustard powder, and then rub in the butter with your fingertips until
the mixture resembles fine breadcrumbs. Stir in the mustard seeds, mint,
and halloumi.

3. Using a spatula, gently stir the beaten egg into the flour and cheese mixture, adding enough milk to form a soft dough. Add more flour or milk, if necessary, to make the dough stick together without being too dry or too wet.

4. Dust a clean surface with flour and gently roll out the dough, about ¾ inch (2 cm) thick. Use a 2½ inch (6 cm) fluted cutter to cut out rounds. Roll out the leftover dough and cut out some more rounds, so you have approximately six scones.

5. Place the scones on the prepared cookie sheet and brush them with milk. Sprinkle with sesame seeds and a little grated halloumi. Bake in the oven for 10–15 minutes until risen and golden brown.

6. Dust the scones with cayenne and let them cool slightly before serving. You can split and butter them, if you like.

# Make your own jam

Jam is a great way to prolong your summer berry harvest, whether you grow raspberries yourself or buy them from a farm stand. If jam is canned correctly, it can be stored safely for months.

## Homemade Raspberry Jam

Raspberry jam is the perfect sweet pick-me-up for
those cold winter mornings, and it makes a great
Christmas gift for your friends and family, too.

*Makes 1 large jar or 2 smaller jars • Prep overnight • Cooking time 35 minutes*

1 lb/4 cups (450 g) raspberries
1 lb/2¼ cups (450 g) coarse-grain white granulated sugar
Zest and juice of 1 lemon

1. The night before you make the jam, macerate the raspberries by combining them with the sugar in a large bowl. Cover the bowl and set it aside.

2. When you are ready to make the jam, put a plate in the freezer. Pour the macerated fruit into a large saucepan, making sure to scrape down all the sugar and juices from the bowl. Add the lemon zest and juice and place the pan over low heat and cook until all the sugar has dissolved. Turn the heat up to high and then simmer for 5–10 minutes until the jam is thick, stirring occasionally to prevent it from sticking.

3. To test if the jam is ready, remove the plate from the freezer and drop a teaspoon of jam onto it. Once it is cool, press the jam with your finger—it should wrinkle. If the jam is too runny, heat it in the pan for a few minutes until you reach the wrinkle stage.

4. Remove the pan from the heat and scrape off any scum from the top. Let the pan cool slightly for 20 minutes, then ladle the jam into one large or two smaller sterilized jars. Seal immediately and allow the jam to cool completely. Store it in a cool, dark place. Once the jar is open, keep it in the fridge.

# How to photograph your food

Once you've prepared your food, it's time to share it with the world on social media! First, you need to make sure you are making the most of natural light. You'll want to set up a food photography area next to a window, where the natural light is soft. You may find the light is too harsh at midday, in which case you should experiment with shooting in the morning or late afternoon. If the light is too strong, there will be very dark shadows and very bright highlights in your image, and it might be difficult to make out the details. Diffused natural light will evenly expose your subject with a gentle glow.

One of the most exciting parts of food photography is styling. With good styling, the camera is almost an afterthought—you can create stunning visuals with your phone camera alone if you get the set-up right. Think about your backdrops. Try to use a surface that isn't too reflective. Old scaffolding planks, reclaimed wood, tabletops, and even specialty food photography backdrops will help create the vibe of a rustic farmhouse kitchen. If you don't have much space for reclaimed wood, you can purchase vinyl food-photography backdrops that roll up into a cardboard tube.

It's always worth keeping an eye out for vintage props while you're in a second-hand store or at a garage sale; they really do add magic to your photographs. Decorate your scene with props such as china saucers, cake stands, interesting glasses, linen napkins, and vintage cutlery. These will help to recreate a rustic setting.

Two of the most popular angles for food photography are overhead and straight on (directly facing the subject). You will notice that some foods will be much easier to shoot from a particular angle. Cake, for example, is often easiest to shoot straight on because of its height. In contrast, a bowl of porridge and berries is often easier to shoot overhead, as this will show details of the food and scene more clearly. Play around with both angles and see which works best for your subject.

Whether you are growing your own produce, stocking up at the local farmers market or checking your supermarket shelves to see what's in season, there's always a way to make the most of your local food supply. Nothing tastes better or is more gratifying to cook than freshly picked fruit and vegetables.

# OUTDOOR
# LIFE

# OUTDOOR LIFE

Beyond life at home, there are plenty of other ways we can bring a little bit of Cottagecore into our experience through the great outdoors. You may be interested in hiking and outdoor sports. Perhaps you enjoy walking your dogs through woodlands and meadows? Or maybe you simply enjoy the peaceful feeling of noticing the fresh air on your skin.

Green spaces allow us to get back in touch with the simple things and connect with nature. Research has shown that the presence of green spaces in urban settings reduces stress and anxiety and prolongs life expectancy via increased physical activity and improved mental health. It's no wonder ecotherapy is becoming a popular means of tackling the stress of modern life. There have even been studies on green micro-breaks, showcasing the incredible healing power of taking a technology-free, short break in a green space.

# Forest bathing

Forest bathing is a Japanese relaxation technique, known in Japan as *shinrin yoku*. It is an act of mindfulness. Through the simple act of observing nature under a canopy of trees, there are a number of positive effects on the body, including reduced stress, lowered blood pressure, and increased immune function. The positive effects of forest bathing are so well documented that a number of doctors have started recommending the practice as a means of boosting patients' wellbeing.

If you enjoy woodland trails, or perhaps walk a dog regularly, you may wonder whether you have unintentionally enjoyed the act of forest bathing. However, one key feature is intentionality—going into the forest or a green space with relaxation in mind. This means a distraction-free visit. No dogs, no phones, and no rush.

Once you have eliminated any distractions, you can be guided entirely by your senses. Pay attention to what you see, hear, and smell. Instead of following a map, follow your senses with curiosity, and take everything in. Beyond relaxation, there is no agenda.

Beginners may find a guided forest-bathing session helpful. When you first pay attention to your sensory experience, distraction is inevitable, but a guide will help you return your attention to your senses. They may slow down your walking speed or direct you to a particular pattern or texture.

# Here are some tips for self-guided forest bathing:

1.  Choose a quiet wooded location, outside of peak visiting times if possible.

2.  Allocate two to three hours so that you don't feel rushed (though note that a few minutes of practice is still beneficial, if you are pressed for time.)

3.  Turn off your phone and put it out of immediate reach in a pocket or bag.

4.  Slow down your walking speed—and remember, this is an act of observation rather than exploration.

5.  If you find a comfortable place to sit, take a seat. Being still may encourage birds and other observable wildlife to enter the area.

6.  Work through your senses one by one. What can you hear? Are there any textures you want to touch? What do they feel like? Can you feel warmth or fresh air on your skin?

7.  Check how you're breathing. If it's fast, try taking a few deep breaths to slow down the rhythm. This will help you feel more relaxed.

# Foraging

A popular theme in the Cottagecore esthetic is collecting food from the wild, better known as foraging. Heading into the wild with a small woven basket is reminiscent of fairy tales and has become a popular part of the escapism that Cottagecore has to offer.

There are plenty of foods we can collect from the wild, as long as we treat nature responsibly in the process. It's also essential to pick plants that are safe. Some wild foods, such as mushrooms, can be poisonous and hard to identify (never eat anything you can't identify). Make sure you take photographs and descriptions with you, and if you are in doubt about something, don't eat it.

The most obvious value of foraging is the result—free food—although there is also an immense benefit to be gained from exploring nature, paying attention to the details of seasonal change, and enjoying your own presence in the great outdoors. Foraging allows us to think about where our foods come from and how they fit into the natural world. If you enjoy foraging, you may also wish to support an organization that protects native woodlands, in order to give something back to nature.

The following is a basic guide; it's worth looking into foraging in your local area, too, as different regions will have differing landscapes. Again, remember to take a guide or other image references with you to make sure you are picking safe foods, respect the guidelines of landowners and endangered species lists, and be sure that the plants you are picking haven't been sprayed with chemicals.

# Spring foraging

As nature reawakens from her winter rest, there are lots of wild foods to be found in spring.

### Dandelions

Dandelions are easy to identify and are widespread in meadows, gardens—and your backyard. Look for the bright yellow rosette of petals. All parts of the dandelion are edible and can be used either raw or cooked as part of a recipe. Try making dandelion honey or dandelion tea with the yellow flowers, or a salad with the young leaves.

### Nettles

Nettle, or stinging nettle, is another common plant. Though it is sometimes considered a weed, nettle is in fact a superfood that has been used for centuries as an herbal medicine. Pick nettle leaves with gloves to avoid getting stung. You could try nettle tea or soup or even sautéed nettles as a side dish.

### Wild garlic

Wild garlic can be found in damp and shady woods. You'll know when you've found it thanks to its strong aroma. Both the leaves and flowers of wild garlic are edible, but you'll find the most efficient method is to collect as many leaves as possible. Wild garlic is a versatile ingredient. You may want to try making wild garlic pesto, butter, or bread.

# Summer foraging

Many plants are at their best in the summer, when berries and edible flowers are in abundance. There is a bountiful harvest for those who venture into nature with a basket.

## Elder

When using elder, you want to be sure to use only the flowers and berries (the rest of the tree is toxic). Elderflower has a beautiful, fresh flavor and scent, and is great in teas, syrups, and liqueurs.

## Wild strawberries

If you're not able to grow your own strawberries, fear not! You can find wild ones growing in open fields, woodlands, and even your backyard. It's unlikely you'll get a large harvest, though, so enjoy eating wild strawberries as you pick them straight from the plant.

### Blackberries

Foraging for blackberries is popular among foragers—and for good reason. There are plenty of these delicious berries to be found in unkept areas, like fence rows and along the edge of wooded areas, so you should be able to fill a basket with ease. Blackberries are rich in vitamin C and are great in juices, crumbles, and pies.

## Autumn foraging

As flowering comes to an end and trees shed their leaves, many plants continue to bear edible fruits that are a treat to forage.

### Blackthorn

If you are out on an autumn walk, you may come across blackthorn bushes covered in thorns and bright blue fruit (drupes) called "sloes," which can be used to make wine and gin or jam and jelly. You can also use the leaves of the blackthorn bush to make tea.

### Wild raspberries

You may come across wild raspberries in wooded areas in early autumn. If you are lucky enough to find a large crop, you can use them as you

would store-bought berries. If the crop is small, enjoy eating them right off the bush as a fresh and tasty snack.

## Winter foraging

Though winter is the most difficult season for foraging, there are still wild foods to collect. If you know what to look for, you can find a rewarding harvest.

### *Sweet chestnut*

Chestnuts are a festive favorite, and a large tree should give you a plentiful crop. Try roasting chestnuts over an open fire for a tasty Christmas tradition. Alternatively, you may want to try adding them to salads or stuffing.

### *Hairy bittercress*

Though typically considered a weed, hairy bittercress is a peppery herb that makes a fantastic addition to salads and sandwiches. You could also use it to add flavor to pesto or soup.

# Pick your own

If foraging isn't an option, you may be able to find a pick-your-own farm, where you can do the harvesting yourself. Often these are aimed towards young children, but they are becoming increasingly popular with teens and adults too, as more of us are becoming interested in rural pleasures. Picking options run the gamut from flowers and strawberries in the spring to summer blueberries, blackberries, and peaches, all the way to autumn apples and pumpkins.

# Travel guide

Spending more time outdoors allows you to really value the beauty in seasonal change. You can revisit the same spot throughout the year, and each time find a new detail to appreciate. Alternatively, you could curate a travel bucket list based on seasonal details. Here are a few suggestions to get you started.

# Spring

**Bluebells** in Northern Virginia
**Cherry-blossoms** at the **Brooklyn Botanic Garden in New York**
**Tulip farms** in Oregon and Washington

# Summer

**Lavender farms** in Cape Cod, Massachusetts
**English country gardens** in the Cotswolds, England
**Fairy-tale castles** in the Scottish Highlands

# Autumn

**Glorious autumn** color in New England
**Gothic fairy-tale castles** in Rhine, Germany
**Idyllic autumn scenes** in The Great Smoky Mountains,
North Carolina and Tennessee

# Winter

**Snow-covered peaks** in Rocky Mountain National Park, Colorado
**Winter activities** in Banff National Park, Canada
**Christmas** celebrations in Rochefort-en-Terre, France

# Photography tips for the great outdoors

Inspired by historic country living, classic novels, and paintings from a bygone era, outdoor spaces are a fundamental part of Cottagecore imagery. Using the timeless backdrop of nature is perfect for staging a cottage-inspired photoshoot.

The most important point here is to look for locations. Meadows make for a simple but effective scene. Better still, you could seek permission to use a field of wheat or lavender (lavender farms often allow the public to explore during certain hours). You can also look for unspoiled historic towns or villages and let the fabric of the old buildings set the scene for you.

Try to avoid hints of modern life, whether parked cars, crowds of visitors, telephone lines, or modern architecture. If you choose a green space in a city, you might want to look for individual details within it, rather than using the area as a whole—for example, framing your shoot around an ancient tree or a flowering shrub.

As always, light is key. If you want to create a moody feel, take your pictures in the rain or on a grey or overcast day. The most romantic shoots will be in the golden hour after a glorious day of sunshine, or try morning mist for a sense of enchantment. As a general rule, sunshine from lunchtime into early afternoon is the most difficult light to work with. If you find yourself shooting in the middle of a sunny day, it might help to work in dappled light, under a tree perhaps.

Props will help add the finishing touches. If you are creating a travel-themed shoot, you could try using vintage luggage. If you are out foraging, take a woven basket with you and fill it to the brim with wild foods and flowers.

Connecting with nature is at the heart of Cottagecore. Thankfully, there are a number of ways to appreciate the great outdoors. If you are pressed for time or unable to travel, you can still find plenty of joy in observing a green space on your way to work or paying attention to the gardens, trees, and window displays in your neighborhood. Even just a little bit of nature will do your mind a lot of good.

# HERBOLOGY

# HERBOLOGY

Herbs have a longstanding history in cottage life. The earliest cottages would have had some sort of herb garden for entirely practical purposes, and many medicinal uses are still relevant today. A number of these have now been proven by science, while others remain trusty "old wives' tales." Either way, if you find an herbal remedy that improves your experience, it is worth making the most of it. You can grow herbs and medicinal plants in a garden or on a windowsill, or you can buy prepared herbal products in various forms at your local health store.

# A basic guide to herbology

Here is an overview of popular herbal remedies and medicinal plants.

Remember to consult a health professional if you wish to use herbal medicine. Herbal remedies can have side effects and/or interact with over-the-counter and prescription medicines. So always speak with your doctor first.

## Aloe vera

Aloe vera gel has natural cooling and soothing abilities that make it especially useful for treating itching and swelling. As such, it is often used to treat sunburn, insect bites, and eczema. Aloe vera gel can also be used as a natural moisturiser, as it is rich in vitamins C, E, and beta carotene, which are associated with anti-aging.

*How to use:* harvest aloe vera gel from mature plants that are a few years old. Use a clean, sharp pair of scissors or a knife to remove two to three large leaves from the outside of the plant; cut at the base of the stem and make sure the leaves are free of mold. Hold each leaf with the cut end downward and allow any yellow liquid to drain out. Discard the liquid. Wash the leaves and trim off any spikes. Lay the leaves flat and cut off the skin to expose the gel layer. Remove all skin and yellow gel, until you are left with clear gel only. This can be applied directly to the skin as a topical moisturiser or treatment. If you want a smooth application, you can blend the aloe vera gel, and then strain it through a layer of muslin. Apply the liquid directly to the skin and discard the pulp from inside the muslin. Alternatively, aloe vera products can be purchased from health and beauty stores.

## Chamomile

Chamomile is best known for its calming and anti-anxiety properties, though it boasts many other uses, including use as an anti-inflammatory and pain reliever. As a plant, chamomile is a cottage-garden favorite, and you can grow your own with ease for plentiful summer harvests. Preserve your chamomile flowers by hanging them indoors, upside down to dry—this will provide you with a year-round supply.

*How to use:* infuse fresh or dried chamomile flowers in hot water for tea; or for direct healing to swelling, place a handful of chamomile flowers in the center of a piece of fabric, pull the corners together and secure with an elastic band, then dip in water and place against the skin as a compress. Chamomile can also be purchased as an essential oil. After diluting with a neutral carrier oil (see p. 27), you can massage the oil into your skin or add a few drops to your bath.

# Echinacea

Echinacea is a cottage-garden favorite for its long-lasting and colorful cone-shaped flowers. Native Americans have used echinacea for centuries to treat a number of ailments. Today it is known for its ability to stimulate the immune system, relieve symptoms of colds and flu, and soothe minor cuts and grazes.

*How to use:* echinacea is available in natural health food stores in tea, tablet, liquid, or ointment form. As various parts of the plant can be harvested, the potency of each product is different, and dosage will vary across individual supplements.

# Feverfew

Feverfew was awarded its name thanks to its early use in treating fevers. Today, it is used in the form of tea or supplements to prevent migraines and arthritic pain. It can also be used as an insect repellent. Feverfew may interact with other medications, so be sure to consult a health professional before using it medicinally. With its dense, daisy-like blooms, feverfew is another cottage-garden favorite. Feverfew is easy to grow, dry, and preserve.

*How to use:* if you don't grow your own, feverfew is available in a supplement form from health food stores. Alternatively, you can infuse 1–2 teaspoons of fresh or dried feverfew leaves in a cup of boiling water to brew tea.

# Garlic

Garlic has a number of uses: it improves cholesterol levels, which may help to lower the risk of heart disease; it is used to fight off the common cold, thanks to its dense nutritional value; and it has also been shown

"If country life is healthful to the body, it is no less so to the mind."

– Giovanni Ruffini –

to reduce oxidative stress, which may lower the risk of brain diseases, including dementia. Thankfully, garlic is widely used in the kitchen, so it is quite easy to include in your routine.

*How to use:* garlic can be bought as a supplement from health food stores, although the benefits of these supplements have been contested. Research suggests that garlic cloves are best used fresh, after being cut or crushed. If you can incorporate 5–12 cloves into your daily meals, you will be making the most of it. Garlic is easiest to digest when roasted whole. Roasted garlic has a more subtle and sweet flavor, which you may find more tasty, too: leave the skin on the garlic bulb, slice and discard the top quarter inch or so, then place the bulb on a sheet of foil, drizzle with olive oil, wrap in the foil, and roast in the oven at 400°F (200°C/180°C fan/gas 6) for 30 minutes.

## Ginger

Ginger is well known as an effective remedy for nausea and inflammation, and its ability to soothe the digestive system. It is often used as a remedy for morning sickness in pregnancy and alleviating period pain within the first few days of menstruation. Ginger can also have positive effects on circulation, as well as encouraging perspiration during colds and flu. Ginger root and powdered ginger are readily available in supermarkets and greengrocers. If you save a section of the root, you can plant it in a pot of compost and grow ginger as a houseplant. Once your plant is established, you can harvest more of the roots for consumption.

*How to use:* there are various ways to include ginger in your diet. You can use freshly grated ginger in curries and stir fries, or infuse thin slices in boiling water to brew tea. In cooking, you may find it easier to use powdered or pickled ginger.

## Lavender

Lavender can be used to reduce stress and anxiety, and to encourage sleep. Lavender plants can be grown in a garden or on a windowsill, and then hung upside down to dry. Lavender is also a useful pest deterrent—putting sachets of dried lavender in your closets and drawers can help to discourage pesky moths from eating holes in your clothes, while rubbing diluted lavender oil onto your skin may keep mosquitoes and other biting insects away.

*How to use:* you can use 1–2 teaspoons of fresh or dried lavender flowers in a cup of boiling water to brew a calming tea. Alternatively, you can store dried lavender flowers in a small cotton bag under your pillow to provide a soothing scent at bedtime. You can infuse a jar of neutral oil, such as almond or argan oil with lavender flowers for at least one week, after which the oil will become beautifully scented and can be used as a homemade alternative to lavender essential oil. Alternatively, you can buy the essential oil from a lavender farm or health food store. It will need diluting with a carrier oil before use, however, as it is very potent.

## St John's wort

St John's wort is a wild plant with a long history of use as a natural antidepressant. It is also sometimes used as a treatment for mild anxiety, seasonal affective disorder, and sleep disturbances.

*Note:* St John's wort interacts with many medicines, including antidepressants and birth-control pills, so it should only be taken in conjunction with guidance from a health professional.

*How to use:* St John's wort is available as an over-the-counter supplement in many health food stores.

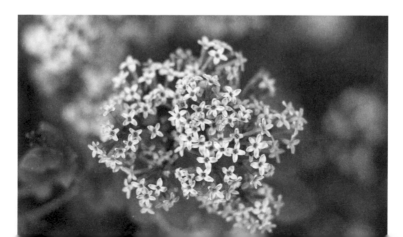

## Tea tree

The tea tree is native to Australia. Its oil can be used as a cleanser and sanitizer, as it kills a number of common bacteria, viruses, and fungi. Tea tree oil is often used as a treatment for mild acne and skin conditions or to cleanse small wounds or insect bites.

*How to use:* tea tree oil can be purchased as an essential oil. As it is highly potent, you should dilute it with a neutral carrier oil before use, particularly if you have sensitive skin. You can also add a few drops of diluted tea tree oil to your bath. Do not consume the oil, and avoid contact with eyes and ears.

## Valerian

Valerian is a wild plant that grows among grasslands. The root is dried and used as a sleep aid and relaxant; it was used historically in ancient Greece and Rome to treat headaches and trembling.

*How to use:* the easiest way to use valerian root is to purchase a tea blend with valerian as an ingredient. If you look for bedtime teas in health food stores you are likely to find one. Alternatively, you can purchase dried valerian root and infuse 1–2 teaspoons in a mug of boiling water to make your own tea. Consume this about one hour before sleeping.

# Easy herbs to grow for tea

There are plenty of easy-to-grow herbs that can be used to make a cup of tea. To preserve your harvest, hang a bunch of your home-grown herbs upside down from the ceiling to dry out. This will supply you with herbal teas until the next harvest season.

Your tea can be made with either fresh or dried herbs. To make it, simply infuse 1–2 teaspoons of one of the following herbs in a mug of boiling water and enjoy it when it reaches a comfortable temperature. The part of the plant that is most commonly used in herbal remedies is in parentheses in the list below:

* Chamomile (flowers)
* Fennel (seeds)
* Feverfew (leaves)
* Lavender (flowers)
* Lemon balm (leaves)
* Peppermint (leaves)
* Rosemary (leaves)

All the plants above can grow in pots and will reflower year after year.

Hopefully, you have found an herbal tea or remedy to grow or enjoy. Herbs and plants hold incredible properties—from early cottage gardens to modern medical usage, it's no wonder they have such a longstanding medicinal history.

# MAGICK AND ENCHANTMENT

# MAGICK AND ENCHANTMENT

There is an air of enchantment within Cottagecore. For some, this means a journey into the world of magick and witchcraft. For others, it means taking inspiration from fairy tales and fantasy in the way they view the world.

The realms of magick and witchcraft are rich and wonderful to explore. You might try your hand at tarot reading or crafting spells, or perhaps pay attention to the cycles of the sun and the moon, and the way these affect your mind and body, and nature around you.

You might wish to follow a more general path towards enchantment; through noticing details in nature, finding simple pleasures, and nourishing your inner child.

# Magick

The term magick, with a "k," is widely used to differentiate the practice of spiritual magick from the card tricks and staged illusions that we have grown to associate with the term "magic." Many of those who practice magick believe in karma—the notion that "you get what you give." In this case, spells are not used to cause harm, as an individual can bring harm upon themselves through their own maladaptive choices. Magick is a neutral term—in itself, it is neither good nor bad—the intention being determined by those who practice it.

Magick practiced outside of Wicca is tailored to the individual. There are no firm rules on how it is used, and many practitioners will also abide by another religion. For many young people, magick provides freedom of expression and an escape from rigid social "norms."

The beauty of this approach is that you are free to explore as many or as few approaches as you'd like. Here are a few ideas to introduce you to magick.

## Dream journal

As soon as you wake up, if you remember your dream, write it in a journal. This helps you to tap into your subconscious thoughts. You will be able to understand your deepest desires, hopes, fears, and insecurities. The more you do this, the more likely you will be to remember your dreams in future.

# Equinox and solstice

Equinox and solstice are astronomical occurrences that determine
seasonal transition. During equinox, the sun is directly above the Equator,
meaning night and day are of equal length. In solstice, the sun's path is
at its furthest point from the Equator. Winter solstice is the shortest day
of the year, while summer solstice is the longest. Witches, who live by the
cycle of the sun and moon, celebrate Equinox and Solstice with spiritual
rituals, such as creating trays or offerings, reading poems, and meditating.

# Casting spells

Casting a spell can help you to set your intentions and work towards
your goals. You can source spells online or from books, or you can make
your own basic ones. If you've ever made a wish over a birthday cake,
you've cast a spell before. Think about your goal—for example, you may
want to achieve greater self-acceptance. Summarize your desire in a few
words—such as, "I will learn to love and accept myself"—then repeat your
sentence in a way that feels meaningful to you. This might be writing it
down, speaking to yourself in the mirror, or rehearsing over candlelight.

# Tarot reading

Tarot cards are a deck of seventy-eight cards that are used as a tool for
divination. Each card has a meaning that can be applied as a framework
for understanding your intuition. Though there is a complex structure

to tarot readings, the basic format is as follows: you ask an open-ended question to the deck of cards and use the reading to guide you forward. For example, you may ask, "What should I look for in a relationship?" or "How can I move away from feeling stressed?" You will then shuffle the deck and pull out one or multiple cards. Let the cards speak to your intuition and guide you through your question. Tarot readings are a useful tool for reflection and interpreting possibilities.

# Enchantment

Cottagecore imagery often evokes a sense of enchantment and fairy tales. It is a form of escapism, but it also seeks to bring fantasy into the everyday and provide a real sense of wonder. There are plenty of ways to let a little bit of enchantment into your life; here are just a few.

## Escape into fairy-tale locations

This might be a woodland walk, or a visit to an unspoiled historic village, a castle, or even your local pumpkin patch. Any of these places can evoke a fairytale image. It might sound a little cheesy, but these locations can really get your imagination running wild, providing an alternative fantasy, and a doorway to escape modern stress.

## Nourish your inner child

As we grow older, we are increasingly laden with demands, chores, and responsibilities. Under the weight of it all, it's easy to lose sight of your inner child. Think of the things that used to bring you joy—they are still pathways to happiness today. Try to let go of the idea that you're too old for something. If you want to jump in puddles on a rainy day, you go and enjoy it! Sing and dance to your favorite songs like nobody is watching, go on fairground rides, and look forward to that bag of candy.

"The world is full
of magic things
patiently waiting
for our senses
to grow sharper."

– W. B. Yeats –

# Cherish your hobbies

There is so much pressure to excel at a hobby that we can be put off even trying to have one in the first place. There is also an expectation to monetize our hobbies, so that we can be the textbook definition of "successful." If you can defy those demands, and practice something simply for the love of doing it, it will bring you an uplifting sense of purpose and wonderment. If you are lucky enough to have a hobby already, cherish it and protect it from outside influences. If you haven't found one yet, allow yourself the space to try a new craft or experience without judgement or expectations. Crafts such as knitting, which involve repeating and rhythmic movements, can be incredibly calming.

Everyone is different, and there is no right or wrong way to let a bit of magick or enchantment into your life. Practicing magick can help to provide the sense of escapism that is central to Cottagecore, while writing and casting spells can help you to focus on your goals and self-development. Experiment with the possibilities until you find a structure that works for you.

# CULTURE

# CULTURE

The desire to return to a simple way of living is everywhere. Previously, popular culture might have focused on hustle and the American dream, but now there is more of an emphasis, at least in some places, on becoming gentler and living a more pastoral life. Forget wealth and conventional success—our new aspirations are freedom, self-expression, and a love of the natural world.

So those with a bookish streak might want to have a cozy evening curled up with a Jane Austen novel. If film is more your cup of tea, many classic tales have been bought to life on screen, and the elaborate artistry, set, and costume design create a totally immersive and enchanting world that's sure to satisfy your penchant for Cottagecore. If you find yourself wanting some culture on the go, why not add a little magic to your journey with a Cottagecore playlist?

# Music

Cottagecore playlists often appreciate indie folk artists and songs that comment on the wilderness, fairy tales, and emotional experiences. If you're in search of some new Cottagecore music, here are some artists to listen to:

## Taylor Swift

Singer-songwriter Taylor Swift channelled Cottagecore's magic in her album, *Folklore*. Unlike her usual pop style, it is a mellow album structured on gentle piano and guitar. Her lyrics tell a collection of imagined stories, with recurring character arcs and themes of love, whimsy, and escapism woven through the album. In true Cottagecore spirit, Swift described the writing process of *Folklore* as "escaping into fantasy."

## Sufjan Stevens

Sufjan Stevens is a singer, songwriter, and multi-instrumentalist living in New York City. He has a remarkable ability to move between instruments and themes, so his music is hard to categorize, although it is often linked to indie folk or alternative rock. Songs such as "Mystery of Love" and "Should Have Known Better" are favorites among Cottagecore playlists, as they guide us gently through themes of love, grief, and spirituality, providing a space to confront raw emotion.

## Joanna Wang

Singer–songwriter Joanna Wang is inspired by a mix of pop, video games, and fairy tales. Covers like "Alice in Wonderland," "Moon River," and "Pure Imagination" are sure to make you feel some Cottagecore magic.

## Lord Huron

Lord Huron is an indie folk band based in Los Angeles. Lead artist, Ben Schneider, named the band after his childhood memories of visiting Lake Huron. The band is a tribute to escaping into the wilderness, finding freedom in nature, and playing music around a campfire. Their first full-length album, *Lonesome Dreams*, is a collection of nostalgic adventure tales told through music. If you're looking for a Cottagecore road-trip playlist, start with Lord Huron.

# Cottagecore playlist

* "Cardigan"—Taylor Swift
* "Meet Me In The Woods"—Lord Huron
* "Alice in Wonderland"—Joanna Wang
* "Mystery of Love"—Sufjan Stevens
* "Fast Car"—Tracy Chapman
* "The Secret Garden"—AURORA
* "Youth"—Daughter
* "Little Talks"—Of Monsters and Men
* "Dog Days Are Over"—Florence + The Machine
* "I Follow Rivers"—Lykke Li
* "Sunlight"—Hozier
* "Bloom"—The Paper Kites

# Film

Cottagecore film lovers will most likely be drawn to modern re-imaginings of classic literature—from their elaborate historic costumes and styling to the picture-perfect locations, stripped of all hints of modernity. Here are some recommendations for your next movie night.

## *Little Women*

The classic novel *Little Women* by Louisa May Alcott has been retold through film in 1949, 1994, and 2019. All versions are beautiful in their own right and deserve to be recommended. The 2019 version has some especially breathtaking scenery, effects, and costume design. We follow the four March sisters as they chase their dreams, in spite of life's hardships. Within no time, you feel like you are part of their family, sharing every step of their emotional journey.

## *Moonrise Kingdom*

A Cottagecore film guide would not be complete without a little Wes Anderson. *Moonrise Kingdom* tells the story of adolescent love, and the desire to escape the stresses of modern life by running away into the wilderness. With classic Wes Anderson artistry, dreamy pastel hues, and perfectly styled 60s outfits and props, this is a film that will inspire your creative side.

"I declare after all there is no enjoyment like reading! How much sooner one tires of any thing than of a book!—When I have a house of my own, I shall be miserable if I have not an excellent library."

– Jane Austen –

## *Pride and Prejudice*

There have been a number of adaptations of Jane Austen's *Pride and Prejudice*, including a 1995 TV series and a 2005 film. There has been an ongoing debate among fans as to which of these two versions does the most justice to the novel, though they are both wonderful in different ways. The 2005 version features Keira Knightley as Elizabeth Bennet and includes fabulous Cottagecore-esque locations, including Groombridge Place, Chatsworth House, and Stourhead, brought to life with breathtaking cinematography. Those with an eye for historic fashion will also enjoy the Regency costumes. There is a lot to be inspired by.

### Other Cottagecore film recommendations

* *Fairytale: A True Story* (1997)

* *Picnic at Hanging Rock* (1975)

* *A Room With a View* (1985)

* *My Neighbor Totoro* (1988)

* *The Secret Garden* (1993 & 2020)

* *Mary and the Witch's Flower* (2017)

# Reading

You can always count on a classic if you want to cozy up under the covers with a book. Here are a few you can try if you want to escape into a fantasyland of nature and whimsy.

## *The Secret Garden*

This novel by Frances Hodgson Burnett has remained a favorite among children since it was published in 1911. Set in England, the novel's overarching theme is the rejuvenating power of nature. As the characters spend more time in the natural landscape, their health and imaginations flourish, and as nature cares for them, they, in turn, care for the secret garden. It is a whimsical tale of friendship and magic—a classic not to miss.

## *Alice's Adventures in Wonderland*

Chances are you are already familiar with the modern adaptations of *Alice in Wonderland*. The original work, *Alice's Adventures in Wonderland*, is a novel by Lewis Carroll, published in 1865. We follow Alice on a journey into a fantasy land, where she meets an assortment of interesting creatures. The novel brings a deeper experience of childhood innocence, and pokes fun at the arbitrary and sometimes unnecessary complexities of adult life. It is a reminder to listen to our inner child.

## *Wuthering Heights*

Written by Emily Brontë and published in 1847, *Wuthering Heights* is often cited as the greatest love story, although it doesn't portray love in the way you might expect. Love in *Wuthering Heights* is wild, psychotic, and haunting. This book is raw and eerie, inspired by the landscape of the Yorkshire moors.

### Five more books to add to your Cottagecore reading list

1. *Anne of Green Gables* by L. M. Montgomery

2. *The Wind in the Willows* by Kenneth Grahame

3. *World of Wonders: In Praise of Fireflies, Whale Sharks, and Other Astonishments* by Aimee Nezhukumatathil

4. *The Secret Life of Bees* by Sue Monk Kidd

5. *Little House in the Big Woods* by Laura Ingalls Wilder

There are plenty of vintage works to provide the backbone to Cottagecore culture. Now, as we reinvent what it means to embrace pastoral aspects of life, there are lots of modern interpretations of Cottagecore, too.

# ENTERTAINING

# ENTERTAINING

Once you've welcomed Cottagecore into your own experience, why not share the joy with your loved ones, too? Cottagecore is about connection, be it with nature, with yourself, or with your loved ones. To host the perfect Cottagecore get-together, think all things whimsy and pastoral. A picnic nestled amongst the trees, an assortment of eclectic vintage props, a centerpiece of homemade baked goods and, most importantly, the company of treasured friends. With a bit of preparation, you can create a tea party fit for a fairy tale.

So from a quiet cup of herbal tea with a friend to an elaborate garden party with a welcome crowd, here are some ways to come together in true Cottagecore spirit.

# Baking

Sharing homemade cake is a win-win. Not only do you get to enjoy the comfort and nostalgia of baking, you also get to show your loved ones you care.

## Honey And Almond Cake

This honey and almond cake is delicious with a cup of tea, and also makes a fabulous centerpiece for a grander occasion.

*Serves 8 • Prep 15 minutes • Cooking time 35–40 minutes*

7 oz/¾ cups (185 g) almond butter

4 oz/9 tablespoons (113 g) butter, at room temperature

6 oz/½ cup (180 ml) clear honey, plus extra for drizzling

2 medium free-range eggs, beaten

4¼ oz/1 cup (120g) all-purpose flour

1 tsp baking powder

½ tsp baking soda

½ tsp salt

3 oz/¾ cup (75 g) ground almonds (almond meal)

3–4 tbsp sliced almonds

1. Preheat the oven to 350°F (180°C/160°C fan/gas 4). Line an 8-inch (20-cm) springform pan with parchment paper.

2. Using a food processor or electric hand mixer, beat the almond butter, butter, and honey until smooth and well combined. Whisk in the beaten eggs.

3. Sift the flour, baking powder, and baking soda into the mixture. Add the salt and gently fold in the ground almonds with a metal spoon, using a figure-of-eight motion, until everything is evenly incorporated.

4. Spoon the mixture into the lined baking pan and sprinkle the sliced almonds over the top. Bake in the preheated oven for 35–40 minutes, until the cake is risen and golden brown and springs back when you press it gently. To test whether it's cooked, insert a metal skewer into the center—if it comes out clean, it's ready.

5. Let the cake cool in the pan for 10 minutes before turning it out onto a wire rack. Drizzle some honey over the warm cake and let it sit until it is completely cool and has absorbed all the honey. Cut into slices to serve. Store in an airtight container for up to 5 days.

# How to throw
# a tea party

A tea party is a wonderful way to celebrate a birthday or special occasion. You may want a simple tea-and-scones affair, or perhaps you want to go full blown into Alice-in-Wonderland territory.

First, assess the basic structure. If you are blessed with good weather, make sure you have picnic rugs and a hamper to stage your tea party. An outdoor table and chairs also make for an enchanting setting, particularly if you have a vintage metal or wooden set. Consider covering your table with a crisp white tablecloth, if you are hosting a formal event, or a chintzy floral fabric for a more relaxed vibe.

Next up is crockery. The quintessential set-up here is the three-tiered plate stand, a large teapot, accompanied by individual teacups and saucers and finally, a set of vintage cutlery. If you don't have a plate stand, a selection of mismatched vintage plates can be just as charming. Chances are, you'll be able to find a good selection in a second-hand store.

You will probably find that a lot of your table or picnic-rug space is occupied with food and drink, so decorations can be kept simple—a small pitcher of fresh or dried flowers is perfect.

When it comes to the food, the menu for a full afternoon tea usually consists of savory finger sandwiches (no crusts!), scones with cream and jam, and a platter of desserts, including cookies, fruit, and miniature cakes. For a lighter, more informal tea, stick with scones, cream, and jam.

Food should be accompanied by tea. You can get creative here. There are plenty of gorgeously fragrant loose-leaf teas to choose from. Classic teas for the occasion include Earl Grey, Assam, and chamomile, but why not also try some floral ones, such as lavender, rose, or elderflower?

If you are celebrating a special occasion, accompany your afternoon tea with a garden punch or rosé cocktail. The following recipes may give you some inspiration:

# Gardener's Punch

*Serves 7*

4 oz/½ cup (125 g) superfine sugar

4 oz/½ cup (120 ml) water

¼ oz/½ cup (10 g) fresh basil

26 oz/3 cups (750 ml) chilled London dry gin

8 oz/1 cup (250 ml) chilled peach schnapps

26 oz/3 cups (750 ml) chilled peach nectar

8 oz/1 cup (250 ml) freshly squeezed lime juice

32 oz/1 quart (1 litre) chilled soda water

Lime slices, peach slices, raspberries, basil and mint leaves, to garnish

1. Start by making the basil syrup: combine the sugar and water in a small saucepan. Gently heat, stirring until the sugar dissolves. Bring to a boil, then turn down the heat and simmer for 2 minutes. To infuse the syrup, take the pan off the heat, drop in the basil, and let the mixture cool. Strain the syrup into a sterilized jar, discarding the basil, then seal and store in the fridge for up to 2 weeks.

2. Pour all the basil syrup into a large pitcher or punch bowl. Add the gin, peach schnapps, peach nectar, and lime juice and stir to mix well. Top off with soda water. Add slices of lime and peach, a few handfuls of raspberries, and a couple handfuls of basil and mint leaves.

3. Give the mixture a gentle stir and then pour or ladle it into punch glasses. Keep an ice bucket on hand for people who want their punch a little chilled.

# Sloe Gin Fizz

*Serves 1*

2 oz/¼ cup (60 ml) sloe gin
2 tbsp freshly squeezed lemon juice
½ tbsp simple syrup (see p. 192)
Ice cubes, to fill shaker

Soda water, to top off
A lemon wedge and mint sprig, to garnish

1. Pour the sloe gin, lemon juice, and simple syrup into an ice-filled cocktail shaker. Shake together well.

2. Fill a tall glass with ice, strain in the gin mix, then top off with soda water for the fizz. Garnish with the wedge of lemon and sprig of fresh mint.

# English 75

*Serves 1*

1½ oz (45 ml) Earl Grey gin
½ tbsp elderflower cordial
1 tbsp freshly squeezed
lemon juice

2½ oz/⅓ cup (75 ml) English
sparkling wine, chilled

1. Fill a shaker with ice and pour in the gin, elderflower cordial, and lemon juice. Shake together vigorously, then strain into a flute.
2. Carefully pour in half the sparkling wine and give it a little stir, then top off with the rest of the sparkling wine and serve.

# Sweet Honey Rosé

*Serves 1*

1 tbsp honey
1 tbsp water
1½ oz/3 tbsp
(45 ml) whiskey

Splash of lemon juice
1½ oz/3 tbsp (45 ml) rosé

1. There are no secrets to making honey syrup: combine the honey and water and stir until you get a uniform consistency. It's a simple trick that thins out the honey, just enough to make it easier to mix in cold drinks.
2. Combine all the ingredients in a cocktail shaker filled with ice. Shake well and strain into a chilled cocktail glass.

# Decorating ideas

Once your menu is planned, it's time to start setting the scene. Try some of the following decoration ideas to set a perfect Cottagecore mood for entertaining your loved ones.

## Bunting

You can decorate the edge of your table or the surrounding area with a row of bunting, which often comes in floral or chintz patterns, making it perfect for a cottage-inspired party.

## Centerpieces

A centerpiece brings your tablescape together by providing a focal point. If you are serving a cake for dessert, you could use it as the focal point, until it's time to eat it. A tall cake standing on a rustic log or wooden crate is a classic example. Alternatively, you could try a floral arrangement, or a three-tier cake stand decorated with pine cones and foliage.

## Lighting

If your event is taking place in the evening, you'll want to think about lighting. Thankfully there are many gorgeous ways to light the scene. Well-designed lighting can have a magical effect on the mood. Why not try some of the following?

If your table is positioned under a tree, you could suspend a hanging candle chandelier from a branch above.

Get creative with outdoor fairy lights. Hang them so that they flow between trees, along a balcony, or even suspend them from a clothes line or fence post.

Adorn the table with lanterns, candelabra, or jelly jars filled with tea lights.

## Placeholders

If you are hosting more than a couple of guests, it helps to mark people's spaces at the table with placeholders. These can be super simple. Cut a small piece of cardstock and write your guest's name in calligraphy (if you struggle with this, you can print the name with a pretty font instead). Punch a hole through the top of the card, thread some twine through the hole, and finish with a little bow. You could also thread a small piece of foliage through the bow for a rustic finish.

## Placemats

If you are going for a stripped-back, rustic mood, you can use neutral linen placemats or another natural material, such as cork or wool. If you are going for more of a happily cluttered look, use floral chintz fabric for a bit of cottage charm. The same rules apply if you are using a table runner.

# Napkin holders

You may be able to pick up some vintage, brass-style napkin holders, if you're lucky, from a second-hand store. Otherwise, vintage replicas should be available at kitchen supply stores and online. You can create a simple napkin holder by tying a piece of twine around a rolled napkin, finishing it with a bow, and then threading a small piece of foliage through the bow.

# Table decorations

Thankfully, vintage table decorations are easy to come by when either shopping at a second-hand store or going for a walk in the woods. Look for the following items, and don't worry if they are mismatched—that only adds to the charm:

* Moss
* Pine cones
* Foliage—pine branches are particularly good table decorations
* Leaves
* Flowers, to use either loose or in small glass jars to hold them upright
* Vintage books
* Assorted vintage drinking glasses

There are plenty of ways to throw a Cottagecore gathering. Next time you are due to celebrate a friend's birthday, why not host a garden party instead of going out for drinks?

# FINAL THOUGHTS

Cottagecore is a place where we can escape from the chaos of modern life. Sure, it's a bit of a fantasy for most of us. But that isn't a reason not to indulge in it. In fact, all the more reason for it! When we get wrapped up in the dull monotony of working all week, the best thing we can do to lift our spirits is to indulge in a playful, imaginative state and nourish our inner child.

As much as Cottagecore is booming online, it's important to take a few steps away and disconnect from social media. Spend some time in a green space, feel the earth beneath your feet as you walk through the grass, pay attention to what you can see and hear around you, and form a strong memory that you can revisit when you need to. Breathe. Take a moment to re-engage your connection with nature and disengage from your connections online.

When we do share our Cottagecore moments online, it still qualifies as valid escapism. If you are proud of a pie you baked or you saw a beautiful view on a hike and want to share it with your followers, go ahead and celebrate it, making space for joy. Cottagecore isn't about returning to a technology-free era and living off the land. It's a modern balance. In an ideal world, you can enjoy social media and share the positive or real moments and also be aware of when your phone isn't serving you; then it's time to unplug and engage in something cathartic— whether that's enjoying a craft like knitting or taking a break outside.

Getting in touch with simple pleasures doesn't have to be covered in frills. It can be straightforward. And it can also be radical. You can step away from commercialism in different areas of your life. You might choose to upcycle some planters instead of going to the garden center for new ones. Perhaps you'll start buying your produce from the farmers market instead of the supermarket. Maybe you'll add a patch of vintage fabric to your ripped jeans to keep them going for another year. These simple acts are freeing in so many ways. We can take pleasure in the literal act of making something. But we can go one step further, and appreciate the money saved or diverted away from big businesses by repurposing what would otherwise go to waste, and the resources we avoided exploiting by not buying something new.

By taking these small steps, we are saying no to consumerism and mass production where we can. We are celebrating the alternatives of handmade crafts, makers and artisans, upcycling, second-hand shopping, and building things to last. There is a place between minimalism and consumerism where we may buy just enough (from small businesses or ethical brands), cherish our belongings, repair our damaged goods, pot plants for pollinators, follow more plant-based and seasonal diets, and share things when we no longer have a use for them. In fact, we were already doing a lot of these things before the Industrial Revolution. There's no reason why we can't learn to value them again. You don't have to do it all, nor do you need to do things perfectly. Cottagecore is about living a little slower and with greater intention.

The bigger picture is that we reduce our burden on the world's resources. We look out for the environment and we recognize that as we look out for nature, it looks out for us too. It is a two-way relationship, and the key is in the balance of both give and take.

Importantly, Cottagecore has room for everybody. As a movement that was started by the LGBTQIA+ community, it's vital not to lose sight of the original vision. Cottagecore is a safe space from a world that thinks in oppressive categories and binaries. It's a place where experiences are heard and honored, and mistreatment is not welcome. It is a retreat, where you can escape from hardship and nourish yourself, while the rest of the world catches up. If you find the space to heal, you will be stronger when you return.

There is no checklist to prove your worthiness here. At its most straightforward level, Cottagecore is enjoying your commute to work or getting excited about a new houseplant. You might be dreaming about moving to a historic home in the countryside one day, but you might also not! You are allowed to appreciate the city and the countryside, or one and not the other. It's your vision, and you can shape it in a way that best meets your needs.

Have fun experimenting with something new or returning to a lost family tradition. Savor the experience and learn to see meaning outside of conventional wealth and productivity. There is value in existing, observing, and feeling. Get carried away with the fantasy and enjoy your escape into Cottagecore.

*My Cottagecore Journal*

# What will you let go of today?

# What is your favorite season, and what do you like about it?

# When was the happiest time of your life?
## What made it so happy?

# What are your favorite flowers or plants? What is it that draws you to them?

# Describe a time when you felt truly at peace.

# List five things that made you smile today.

1 _____

2 _____

3 _____

4 _____

5 _____

**Head out to your backyard or local park.
Look around at the trees, flowers, and
wildlife—all co-existing in the same space.
How does it make you feel?**

You enter a building and see two rooms. One is full of people chatting, with music playing. The second is empty, except for an armchair and a copy of your favorite book.

Which room do you enter and why?

_____

_____

_____

_____

_____

_____

# What book do you wish you could read again, as if for the first time?

If you could only listen to one album for the
rest of your life, what would it be and why?

# What did you dream about last night?
## How did it make you feel?

**If you could travel anywhere in the world, where would you go—and why?**

# List ten things that make you feel grateful.

1 

2 

3 

4 

5

6 _____

7 _____

8 _____

9 _____

10 _____

# Acknowledgments

Thank you to the team at HarperCollins for your help in putting this book together, particularly Omara for your in-depth guidance and encouragement along the way.

I am forever grateful to my grandad, who showed me the escapism within nature and gardening from an early age.

Thank you to my wonderful partner Aaron and my friends Kym, Tor, Rach, Amy, K, and Andy. Last but not least, thank you to my family–Dad, Kiara, Sue, Shane, and the Wilsons.

# About the Author

Ramona is an influencer and photographer from Somerset, England. She documents cottage life and the English countryside on her Instagram account, @monalogue. In her spare time you'll find her in the garden, where she grows a variety of vegetables and cut flowers. Ramona graduated from the University of Bristol with a degree in Experimental Psychology.